Grown & Virtuous:

28 Simple Lessons To

Unveil the Spiritual Diva in You

Joy C. Daniels

NURTURED SOUL THERAPY, LLC | CHARLOTTE

This book is dedicated to the powerful women and girls in my life:

My sweet mom, Bobbie Irby Hasberry, for being a wellspring of love that always overflows. Your love will not return to you void.

My beloved daughter, Joie C. Hasberry, for grounding me and helping to get direction for my life. I hope that you become all God has destined for you to become; because of me, and in spite of me.

My loving daughter, Yashi E. Hasberry Humphrey, for always being my sunshine on a cloudy day. Always walk in God's light and continue to shine wherever you go.

My gracious grandmother, Margaret Irby, for being a living example of grace, patience, courage, and virtuous living. I appreciate you.

My generous aunt, Claudette Irby DeWitt, who has always had such a giving spirit. I pray you continue to receive the Lord's blessing and the inheritance He has in store for you.

My loyal godsister, D. Joi Falana, for never-ending love and support and always having my back. May all of your most vivid dreams come true.

My amazing friend, Donna D. Jones, for listening to my ranting and knowing just what to say…and not what to say. May you get all that your heart desires.

My fabulous friend, Lanita G. Wimberly, for crackin' my side…always! And for being the best roomie ever! You are my lifelong sister-friend and confidante. "Trust in the Lord WITH ALL YOUR HEART…in all ways acknowledge Him and He will direct thy paths." Remember, He will supply ALL of your needs, according to His riches and glory.

I love you all!

And to all the glorious sistas out there who are strong enough, brave enough, good enough, beautiful enough, and powerful enough and don't even know it yet! Now is YOUR time! This is for YOU!

TABLE OF CONTENTS

WORDS HURT: A Lesson in the Power of Words over Feelings

1

"Sticks and stones may break my bones, but words will never hurt me." ~ Unknown

True…and not true. Let's consider this: Lizzie and Keke, two little girls, are playing the dozens. Lizzie says to Keke, "Your mama is sooooo fat that…." Then Keke responds to Lizzie with, "Well, your mama is sooooo ugly that…." Initially, it started as a fun game. But, Lizzie's mother really may be (perceived) ugly, so she begins to take these jokes personally, gets defensive, and then lashes out very mean-spirited at Keke. Keke, sensing the change in Lizzie, also becomes defensive, and a fight ensues. Isn't this how it really happens?

So, let's look at what happened. Both children were light-hearted at first. Both children also had issues they were dealing with, possibly issues of acceptance or self-esteem. When Lizzie's nerve got struck, she was hurt, that is, she felt pain, and possibly embarrassment or shame. Because we know that "hurt people hurt people," she wanted to hurt her friend the same way she was hurting, so she went on the attack. Keke may have felt confusion, hurt, and then anger at the change in her friend's behavior, and chose to defend herself against the attack by launching an attack of her own.

Now tell me, what did this solve? Absolutely nothing. Did you understand this story? Have you seen kids behave like this? Sure! We all have. Now, imagine adults behaving like that. Worse yet, remember when YOU last behaved like that. Come on, it's time to get real with yourself, and you're not the only one. You got mad recently because someone said something to you that you felt "disrespected" you or "hurt" you or "made you mad." Why did it have that effect on you? *Because you allowed what they said to hit an unhealed place of hurt in you.* So, what should you do?

This is where it starts to get good. When you are feeling those negative feelings, start to train yourself to examine what's going on with you. Look at all the feelings you are feeling: pain, embarrassment, shame, anger, rejection, resentment, jealousy, etc. Then think about WHY you feel that way. Then, dig deeper as to why THAT is the case and WHY you are internalizing what the person said. Then, consider whether it really is a reflection on YOU or not. If it is, is it something you can change or improve? Or, if it's not a reflection on you, let it go! We carry so much old baggage. Isn't it time to put some of it down?

Back to the story. Because Lizzie is strongly connected to her mother, and her beautiful mother is considered ugly by some people, her feelings get hurt because she feels that her mother may be hurt by this because she believes this to be her mother's reality, in some way. And if this is her mother's reality in some way, it must be her own reality in some way, since this is her mother (see the association here?). Dig deeper. She may feel that her "ugly" mom is a reflection of herself and other kids will therefore see her as ugly, too. Dig deeper. She sees that ugly kids are picked on, and are not readily accepted by other kids. Now she is afraid that she won't be accepted. She dreads being ostracized by her friends.

Did Lizzie think all of this through initially? Of course not! Do YOU when you are hurt? Most of us just REACT. If we are to grow from these places of pain, we need to first STOP REACTING (that is, stop lashing out, cussing, carrying on and acting like a fool), then recognize that we are in pain. (You ARE human, aren't you? Therefore, you can feel pain. There is freedom in admitting the truth. There is slavery in running from it. Choose freedom.) We must then strive to understand the pain. After we understand it, we must resolve it.

After we have done the hard work of digging deeper and deeper to understand our pain, it's then time to resolve it. We must reach a point where we say, "This is how I have felt. This is how I have behaved. I don't want to feel this way or behave this way anymore. I have felt this way because…. I forgive so-and-so for their part in this. I forgive myself for this. I accept this about myself. No, I haven't been the greatest person. Yes, I have my faults and this is just one of them. Does this make me bad? No. Does this make me human? Yes. Can I learn from this? Yes. The next time I feel like this I will NOT react. The next time I feel like this I will get quiet and figure out the most peaceful response that will ultimately please God in that situation.

And guess what? With practice and prayer, you WILL get better. You will learn to stop taking things personally. You will get to the point where words don't hurt you and you will be able, at that point, to understand where the other person is coming from. That is, you will be able to think beyond yourself to consider another person. That's growth! That's what you want in order to be a better YOU.

With this being the case, consider what YOU say before you say it. If you know that words can hurt (because words have hurt you, before you were healed), you have to know that words can hurt someone else. Don't be a hurt person that intentionally hurts people (see Romans 12:19). Be big enough to be sensitive to other people and strive for peaceful, productive conversation. Use words to uplift, unite, resolve, encourage, comfort, acknowledge, inspire, motivate, clarify, edify, create, educate, coach, and to speak all that is good. Be big enough to grow beyond yourself and bless someone by the words you speak (refer to Matthew 5:44).

[VIRTUOUS STEPS]

1. Think of three things someone has said to you recently that hurt your feelings. Write them down. Consider why these words hurt you so badly. Resolve to heal that pain. Accept yourself for who you are now. Make any changes you need to make in order to grow. Write these changes down. Forgive yourself and forgive them. Vow to behave differently next time something hurtful is said and vow not to take what is said so personally.

2. Think of three things you said to someone that may have hurt their feelings. Write them down. Consider how the other person (people) may have felt. Repent for what you said. Apologize to the person (people) you hurt. Vow to yourself to become more cognizant of what you say to others. Vow to master your words.

3. Remember, if you don't have anything good to say, consider saying nothing at all.

KNOW THYSELF (Plato): A Lesson in Self-Awareness

2

"You got to be in tune with your star player."

~ Katt Williams, Comedian

How many times has someone asked you, "Why'd you do that?" And your response was, "I don't know?" Aside from your Creator, THE most important person you must get to know is YOURSELF. Answer these questions: Who do you serve? What do you do when you are happy? What makes you happy? What do you do when you are sad? What makes you sad? What do you do when you get angry? Do you ever get depressed? Why? Do you ever feel anxiety? What's causing it? Are you fulfilled? What's your favorite thing to do? What are you known for? Does your job reflect your purpose? What is your purpose? What's your best physical feature? What are your spiritual gifts? What do you do when you are under pressure? What do you do when you feel trapped? What do you do when you feel lonely? What energizes you and makes you come alive? Do you always have to have a man? Why?

If you don't know the answers to these few questions, or if your answers reflect immaturity, then you either do not know yourself well, or you've been behaving like a child. For instance, if the question is, "What do you do when you get angry?" and your answer is, "I cuss the bitch out!" then this reflects a certain level of immaturity (socially and spiritually). However, if your answer to this same question is, "I may yell, but I don't participate in any name-calling," then you probably have a good awareness of your behavior (although yelling isn't necessarily good either).

When you truly know who you are, you understand who you are in Christ. You understand that you were created by the love of God, for the love of God. You are aware that your purpose is to express this love in some divine way. You understand that to be depressed or to feel anxiety reflects some form of disconnect between you and your Heavenly Father. When you know yourself, you know that God loves you just the way you are and He only wants the best for you. When you have a healthy sense of self-awareness, you are not a victim of smoking, drunkenness, gluttony, promiscuity, gambling, excessive spending, laziness, etc. This does not mean that you haven't participated in this destructive behavior; it means you no longer participate in it at this point in your life. You don't participate in pity parties. You are strong, yet gentle. You are comfortable with who you are right now, knowing that you can choose to change yourself anytime you desire. You don't make excuses for your shortcomings (and you are well aware of your shortcomings). You accept full responsibility for the person you are today. You have a healthy appreciation for your past because it has brought you to TODAY and has made you the person that you are.

Knowing yourself means that you truly understand what makes you tick. You understand who pushes what buttons and if negative behavior comes from a particular button being pushed, you work to change your behavior to behavior that reflects more of the positive woman you are striving to become. You recognize that bad behavior does not serve you or God (or anyone else for that matter) and only keeps you from becoming the woman you were meant to be (see Proverbs 25:28).

Since you know who seems to provoke you to negativity, in your increasing wisdom, you can choose to either avoid these people, or make a conscious choice and effort to peacefully co-exist with them. You know that being a woman over 21 years of age has very little to do with your chronological age and more to do with you acting like you have some sense—all the time!

Likewise, if swinging at the playground made you happy when you were a child, you may enjoy swinging as an adult. Who says you can't go swinging? Who says you can't climb trees? Who says you can't play in the water at the beach AND get your hair wet? Who says you can't ride the rollercoaster at the amusement park? When you know yourself, you know that sometimes it's the simple, carefree, child-like things that make you happy. These are the experiences that help to replenish your soul.

If you don't know yourself well, I urge you, get to know yourself. Develop a healthy awareness for who you are. Spend some time with yourself. If you know yourself, but don't like yourself, then CHANGE that today! Whatever you did yesterday, is gone. You can make a fresh start today. Spend some time with yourself—go for a walk, draw, paint, color, cook, clean, get a new hairdo, get a mani/pedi, go visit an orphanage, wash your car, play with makeup, go play at the playground, sit quietly flipping through a magazine, enjoy a movie, meditate, start a journal, read the *Holy Bible*, talk to God, soak in the tub—do something you enjoy, then take time to reflect on how you felt doing the things you chose to do with yourself.

[VIRTUOUS STEPS]

1. Pick three negative emotions that you may feel on any given day. Write them down. Think about what caused you to feel that way. Did you behave maturely or immaturely? Did you behave like a Christian or did you

"lose your religion?" How can you behave better next time? Write it down.

2. Pick three positive emotions that you may feel on any given day. Write them down. Think about what caused you to feel that way. Did you behave like a Christian? How can you experience these good feelings more often? How can you help others to feel these good feelings? Write it down.

3. List three healthy activities you enjoyed as a child. How did you feel when you did these activities? Would you do them again? If so, set aside some time to do them again. If not, why not? Don't be concerned about what people think. Let them go on their own journey of self-discovery. This journey is YOURS. Get started!

UGLY FEET: A Lesson in Self-Acceptance

3

"God grant me the serenity to accept the things I cannot change."

~ Reinhold Niebuhr, Theologian

When I was little, I saw pretty women with long toes. Mine were pretty little feet with pretty little toes. I said to myself, "I want long toes, too." So I started pulling on my toes every day. True story! The more I grew, the longer my toes got. Then they got too long. That's when I realized, "I've got ugly feet."

So for years I covered my feet up. No one was going to see those ugly things. And when they were not hidden, I heard the jokes about, "Geez, you got fingers on the end of your feet!" Tehehehe. Whatever.

Then one summer day, during my young adult years, I read or watched something on TV about self-acceptance. It made me think about those parts of my body that I was unhappy with— especially my feet. What I learned was that my feet are a blessing from my Heavenly Father. He gave me these feet. Whatever I did to them was on me, but He gave them to me for a purpose. My feet were great for walking, running, kicking, prancing on tippy-toe, skipping, dancing and countless other things. Then I took a minute to consider what I would do without my feet. It was then that I realized that without my feet, I would not have been able to walk out of many dangerous situations. I would not have been able to run track and develop shapely legs. I would not have been able to walk across my college campus or then go clubbin' with my girls (I probably could have done without the clubbin'.). I would not have felt the ice cold water on my toes at the beach and feel the sand melting back into the ocean, nature's rejuvenating foot massage. I realized then how unappreciative of my feet I had been. I asked God for forgiveness for my unthankfulness and vanity. I gave thanks for my feet and vowed to cherish them and every other part of my body, recognizing that each part was a blessing and given to me for a divine reason (Psalms 139:14-16).

I started to get frequent pedicures, and now I am pleased to say my feet, although funny-looking, are presentable. I have taken care of them; they are free from corns, bunions, and in-grown toenails. My feet serve me well.

So, I say to you: Love and appreciate all of your body parts. They serve you every day. Through abuse and neglect, your body has served you. It is your temple; it houses your spirit. So I say to you, make peace with your body. Make peace with your body and start today to treat it right. Ask God for forgiveness for being unappreciative and for being vain. Give yourself a big hug and say, "I love you," to yourself, especially to the areas of your body you aren't fond of right now. Begin to honor and respect your body.

By honoring your temple and being thankful, you honor your Creator. Show your appreciation by doing the very best you can with what you have. Remember, you, and all of your parts, were created in His love.

[VIRTUOUS STEPS]

1. What parts of your body are you unpleased with? Your hair? Waistline? Feet? Hands? Legs? Consider how your life would be without these body parts or if these body parts were in worse shape than they are now.

2. Now, consider what small or big change you can make to show appreciation for your body. Can you get a more flattering haircut, color, braids, or wig? Can you do sit-ups, crunches, go walking or avoid fatty foods? Can you get a pedicure and/or manicure or do it yourself? Can you shave your legs or "walk it out?" There is something you can do besides suffer in silence or complain to anyone that will listen. Be proactive. Show God and yourself that you can and will be a good steward over your own body and accept yourself the way you are today and vow to change for the better. And if you cannot change that which you dislike, accept it and move on! Appreciate that your imperfection is part of an imperfect you, and you are to grow beyond your shortcomings into a virtuous woman of God! Don't stand in your own way!

DON'T LET THEM SEE THE CRACK OF YOUR BUTT!:
A Lesson in Dressing Virtuously

4

"What a strange power there is in clothing." ~ Isaac Bashevis Singer, Author

Aja is very pretty, everyone says so. She has big, beautiful hazel eyes, a long, graceful neck, a tiny waist, and thick, wavy hair. Even with Aja being so pretty, she still has not met her Mr. Right. One Saturday night she goes out to the club with her girlfriends. She's determined to meet him this night. Dressed in a dress so tight she couldn't breathe using her right lung, and so short you could see what she ate for breakfast, she headed out with her girlfriends.

She had a good time. She danced, drank, and laughed all night long, but she still did not meet her Mr. Right. Soon, it was time to leave. Aja waited inside the club, finishing her appletini, while her friends went to get the car. After finishing her drink, she walked outside and waited at the curb for her friends. She saw a decent-looking man driving toward her in a shiny, black big body Benz. "Hmmmm," she thought. "Could this be him?"

The man stopped in front of her, rolled down his window and then said to Aja, "How much?" Confused, she responded, "How much what?" He said, "How much are you charging for an hour?" Aja's mouth just dropped open.

What kind of attention are you attracting? Are you like Aja, where men believe you're a prostitute because of the revealing way you dress? Or do they seem to believe that because of the way you dress you're giving it away for free?

A virtuous woman dresses attractively, but is careful about what she intends to attract. A virtuous woman dresses respectably. Breasts are fully contained, she can bend over without showing her thong, she can cross her legs without showing too much thigh, and she looks like she can breathe. She wears colors that reflect her moods and personality. She wears styles that are flattering to her figure.

Her clothes are appropriate for her. She does not go to the store to shop for spandex when she is extremely thick and has what people now affectionately call "belly fat." She does not wear a bikini in public that leaves nothing for the imagination. Her attire says, "I care about myself. I value myself. I love myself. I'm not selling my body and I'm not just giving it away either."

What you wear is part of your image. Quite frankly, if you are not a slut, and don't want to be thought of as a slut, or treated like a slut, then don't dress like a slut. Ever. Period. If your image is to be that of a virtuous woman, and you want to be thought of as such, and treated as such, then dress as a virtuous woman (see 1 Timothy 2:9-10).

Back to Aja, she had enough natural beauty to enhance positively. It's sad that she chose to basically "sell sex" instead of letting the real Aja shine through. She will not attract Mr. Right as long as she looks like she's either selling her body or giving it away for free to anything with a pulse. No good man seriously wants a woman who uses her body to attract men. If you don't believe this, find a good man and ask him. In the words of one good man, "I want my woman to be sexy, not trashy."

Consider how you dress for your job. You dress like you want the position, right? So carry this logic over to the other areas of your life. You want to be a wife? Dress for the position. You want to be a teacher? Dress for the position. You want to be a mother? Dress for the position. Sidebar: since we're on motherhood, please don't be a mother that embarrasses her child and herself by going to the child's school showing too much cleavage and the crack of her behind. That certainly is not exhibiting the life of a virtuous woman. It says, "I'm giving it away everywhere I go, even here at this school." Don't do that to your child! Get it together! Okay, I'm off my soapbox again.

[VIRTUOUS STEPS]

1. Think of a time when what you wore got you negative attention. Was there anything wrong with what you wore? If so, what? How could you have dressed more like a virtuous woman?
2. Think of some women whose style is (generally) respectable and maybe even a little sexy sometimes. For example, First Lady Michelle Obama, Actress Angelina Jolie, etc. What do you like about their styles? Why? Is there anything that you would like to adapt to make it your own style?
3. Go through your closet, and as soon as you can, get rid of those clothes that do not reflect the 21st century virtuous woman that you are becoming. You want to be a virtuous woman? Dress for the position.
4. And while you're making over your wardrobe, consider the natural beauty that you have that you can enhance in a positive, fun way. Is it your flawless skin? Your big almond-shaped eyes? Your long shapely legs? Your pretty feet? Your beautiful smile? Your short, curly hair? God has given us all natural beauty. Virtuously share THAT with the world!

ACT LIKE A LADY: A Lesson in Gentleness

5

"Nothing is so strong as gentleness, nothing so gentle as real
strength."
~ St. Francis de Sales, Bishop of Geneva

Many times women equate loud, brash speech with strength.
Some women seem to believe that the louder they are, the more in
your face they are, the more neck rolling they do, the stronger and
badder they seem. They don't seem to realize that this isn't strength
at all. If anything, it's ignorance, and many of us at one time or
another, have been caught up in this ungodly behavior.

I say to you, in order to be a virtuous woman, you must learn
to be gentle. And, I must add, being gentle is not the same thing as
being weak (see 2 Samuel 22:36). Being gentle is being soft-spoken
yet powerful, sweet but not stupid, kind but not a fool, humble,
courteous, calm and thoughtful, possessing a spirit of cooperation for
the greater good, having self-awareness and self-control, and
expressing tenderness and understanding.

This is not to say that a virtuous woman does not enjoy a
hearty laugh or does not yell for her kids to come downstairs for
dinner. This is to say that a virtuous woman is "calm, cool, and
collected" when she is angry as well as when she is feeling good.

Can a woman with a gentle spirit still "get happy" in church? Absolutely! Can a woman with a gentle spirit still let you know that you have crossed the line? Absolutely! Can a woman with a gentle spirit still protect her children with all the fierceness of a lioness protecting her cubs? You'd better believe it! *It's all in the way you carry yourself.*

A virtuous woman is assertive, not passive, aggressive, or passive-aggressive. She is smart enough to know that you can "catch more flies with honey than with vinegar." She goes for what she wants, but she does it with style and with a good heart and a right mind, in a way that pleases God.

Nadeen was once married to a man with a gentle spirit. They moved into a neighborhood where many of the women were loud, aggressive, and confrontational. She was a housewife and these became her new friends. Soon, Nadeen took on some of these negative traits that her new friends possessed. Her husband began to notice that she was not on her "game" as she had been before their move. She began to talk to him like a dog, yelling and screaming at him when she believed he didn't take her out enough, getting up in his face, nagging him about watching sports, calling him terrible names, generally devaluing him just as the other women devalued their husbands. After a year of this treatment, her husband left her. Nadeen moved back home with her grandmother. Her grandmother saw the woman Nadeen had become, so she retrained Nadeen on how to become a woman with a gentle spirit and how to show love, appreciation, and cooperation. She re-taught her the importance of being humble.

Nadeen's husband agreed to start seeing her again. They began dating and he eventually forgave her and learned to trust her again. They reconciled. Once again, they moved away from their comfort zone, but this time, Nadeen had a newfound appreciation for her husband and had learned so many lessons, one lesson being in gentleness. She sought out a church that reminded her of her grandmother's church. She became involved with women's groups in the church that could support her in growing in the direction God wanted her and her marriage to grow in. And, eventually, she was able to lend support to other women in need.

[VIRTUOUS STEPS]

1. Circle all of these adjectives as they apply to you, and be honest! As Dr. Phil says, "You can't change what you don't acknowledge."

    loud talking
    neck rolling
    finger pointing (literal or figurative)
    up in someone's face
    meanness
    rough handling of people or things
    confrontational
    defensive
    name calling
    out of control
    arrogant

2. Now think of how often you behave like the adjective(s) you circled. Are you happy about this behavior? If not, are you ready to change? Consider some of these opposites to the above negative behaviors. These behaviors are actually some examples of gentleness that you want to embody as a virtuous woman.

    soft-spoken
    relaxed body position and function

no finger pointing (literal or figurative)

respect the private space of others

kindness

handling people or things with care and
tenderness

non-confrontational

cooperative

no name calling, addressing people with
respect

self-control

humble

3. Decide which of the above bad behaviors you want to let go, and which of the good behaviors you want to cultivate. Pray about it and go to it! Consciously monitor your behavior and when you feel the bad behavior coming, stop to consider another more gracious way of behaving that will serve God. Keep practicing. You'll get it.

6

"Not that which goeth into the mouth defileth a man; but that which cometh
out of the mouth, this defileth a man." ~ Matthew 15:11, *Holy Bible*

S&#@! D*%#! F@%$! Mutha F$&@! What does all that *really* mean anyway? We want people to believe that we are intelligent women, but we open our mouths to prove that our intelligence (and maybe self-control) is questionable.

So, let's explore some of the reasons for cursing/cussing:

- Anger
- Frustration
- Upbringing
- Possessed
- "It's cool."
- "Everybody does it."
- Limited vocabulary
- Unable to express oneself adequately or appropriately
- The situation "seems to call for it"
- "I've been cussin' all my life"
-

When I was a little girl, my grandmother would tell me that certain things just weren't "lady-like." My mother still says to this day that if your vocabulary is good enough, you should be able to adequately and effectively express your thoughts and feelings without using profanity. Some people may say, "I just can't help myself." Or, they may say, "It just comes out." This implies a lack of self-control.

I believe we can control ourselves a little better than this. Think about it like this: we go to our jobs daily and don't curse our bosses out. But then we turn around and cuss freely at or with our families and friends. So, we won't "defile" ourselves at work, where we have something to lose, but we'll defile ourselves amongst family and friends?

Let's look at this word "defile." Various dictionaries say that this verb means "to tarnish, damage, dull, or desecrate." So, the Bible says that it's not what goes into our mouths that defiles us, but what comes out. Well, there are only a few things that can come out of our mouths, and if you're sick, then one of those things is totally excusable. But, the Bible wasn't referring to that anyway; it was referring to our words, our language, specifically, profanity.

Think about it like this: You're working on becoming a virtuous woman. Such a woman is highly valuable. Then you open your mouth and start "cussin' like a sailor," thereby devaluing yourself and tarnishing your reputation and damaging your character as a virtuous woman. *You devalue yourself by using profane language.* If you don't demonstrate that you value yourself, why would you expect anyone else to value you?

When something is in you, eventually it will come out, one way or another. If you have joy, peace, and laughter inside of you, it will come out. It will show in the way you live your life. Similarly, if you have hurt, resentment, and jealousy inside you, that will come out as well. So, if you want to be a virtuous woman, you must not only deal with what's coming out of your mouth, but what's inside of you as well. If you have any negative, deep rooted feelings, you must deal with them. You must work towards healing. And if it's just that you were ignorant as to how important the use of language is, well, now you know. You've heard that there's "life and death in the tongue," right? Choose to speak life into your reputation, your character, your future. Leave the profanity out of it.

Candice, a wonderful young woman who's active in her church, enjoys teaching Sunday school to the five year-old group. The kids just love her! While out to dinner one night with a group of her girlfriends, Candice was overheard by one of the deacons using profuse profanity. Instantly, her good reputation was ruined. It went from ruined to questionable. The deacon let his presence be known so that Candice would be aware that she had been overheard. She felt pretty bad and wondered what would happen next.

She didn't have to wait long. At the next meeting with the Sunday school teachers, Candice was asked to give up her class for a while. She was told that even though they believed she was a Christian and cared about the children, that her language indicated that she wasn't exactly who they thought the children should be learning the Bible from. They reminded her of this scripture: "Out of the same mouth proceedeth blessing and cursing. My brethren, these things ought not so to be (James 3:10)." And since a little "slip of the tongue" wasn't the problem, but an entire conversation where profanity was used throughout the conversation on her part, it was clear that this was Candice's lifestyle. This lifestyle, as the deacon explained to her, was not what was desired for someone who was to teach Sunday school, particularly to impressionable little children.

Candice was embarrassed. She was upset with herself. She knew better. Upon examining herself, she realized that she was just hanging out talking to friends the way she has for years. She began to wonder how her friends saw her. She's told them that she's a Christian now; that she has stopped doing a lot of the things she used to do, i.e., clubbing, gossiping, etc. But, she still wondered if they really took her desire for change seriously since she still used the same kind of bad language with them. To them, except for a few changes, she probably still seems like the same old Candice. How can she think that she can set an example for the kids and not want to "walk the walk" with her friends? Candice knew that she had to do better. The deacon was right: Christianity does call for a lifestyle change. That change has to include her heart and her mouth.

A word to the wise: You can master all of the other lessons in this book, but unless you master your mouth, you will not become a virtuous woman.

[VIRTUOUS STEPS]

Finish these sentences:

1. I curse/cuss because I feel....
2. When I curse/cuss, it makes me feel....
3. I curse/cuss when I'm with these people: _____
4. I don't curse/cuss when I'm around these people: _____
5. Instead of cursing/cussing, I can say/do _____.

After finishing the above sentences, continue to study scriptures as the ones listed throughout this chapter in order to help the Word sink deeper into your soul. Pray for a healed heart and better language so that only the good and acceptable comes out of you and your mouth.

REPUTATION VS. CHARACTER:
A Lesson in Building Your Reputation AND Your Character

7

"Reputation is what men and women think of us; character is what
God and angels know of us."
~ Thomas Paine, American Pamphleteer

*When you aspire to become a virtuous woman, you must be
concerned with your character first. Your reputation will then take
care of itself.* Think about it: If you become the embodiment of
patience, kindness, joy, peace and several other virtues, and it shows,
you will eventually have the reputation of being a woman with such
virtues. *The reputation of a virtuous woman follows her character.*
("...All my fellow townsmen know that you are a woman of noble
character." –Ruth 3:11)

There was a young woman I went to college with...let's call
her Amira. Amira had the reputation of having sex with a lot of
college guys...a lot. All the guys talked about her. I even heard them
joking about her several times. They all professed to have had sex
with her. Many of the women began to dislike her because she was
known to be "loose" and they wondered if she had been with their
boyfriends, or if she would if she hadn't gotten around to it.

But, honestly, in talking to her, she was a really nice person. At the time, I felt sorry for her because she had such a bad reputation, the worst I had ever heard of. Even then, I thought, "Boy, she's gonna have a hard time living down THAT reputation! How will she ever get married? Who's gonna want her?" She had been called "slut, whore, hussy, ho," and every other name imaginable behind her back by several different people. But then, much to my surprise, she DID find a man who loved her for the goodness she had inside. Hallelujah!

See, somewhere along the way, Amira stopped doing the things that gave her the bad reputation. She spent more time on herself and left people, particularly men, alone. She had been looking for love in ALL the wrong places and I believe she finally realized that. For a moment, she seemingly dropped off of the face of the earth and her name was no longer falling out of people's mouths. It seems it was then that she found herself and her new husband and he apparently knew of her colorful past, understood her, and loved her unconditionally in spite of it.

We all have some skeletons in our closets that color our pasts. There are things that we have done that we are not proud of; and there will always be someone who is willing to remind us of our imperfections and our past reputations. We may have stolen someone's clothes, cheated on some exams, been known as the loudmouth at work, or worse yet, been known as the troublemaker. We may have had the reputation of stealing girls' boyfriends, thinking we're cute, or being "bougie." We may have dressed "slutty" in the past or may have been considered the world's biggest airhead. We may have been known as being "shady" or had a reputation for being "needy." We may even have had the reputation of being a liar, "trailer park trash," or a gold digger, but, the reality is that when you accept your salvation and are born again, you are able to shed the old person and begin anew and develop new character traits, traits that are more becoming of a virtuous woman. The Bible says, "Therefore if any man be in Christ, he is a new creature: old things are passed away; behold, all things are become new." (2 Corinthians 5:17) The beauty with God is that He is a Forgiver of sins. Let Him show you the way. Study the new character traits you want to embody. Study what it is to become a virtuous woman. If you strive to become a virtuous woman with all diligence, you will then become a woman of good character with a new, solid reputation to follow.

[VIRTUOUS STEPS]

1. Decide which is most important to you: reputation or character? (You can DO things to boost your reputation. You can BE the woman of good character that gives you a good reputation.)
2. Finish this statement: "I want to be known for _____."
3. Finish this statement: "When I die, I want to be remembered for_____."
4. Finish this statement: "I want God to say that I am _____."
5. Finish this statement: "I want God to bless me for _____."
6. Consider this: "I am known for _____because I _____ and
   I feel _____ about it."
7. Finish this statement: "The things I do that damage my reputation are _____."
8. Finish this statement: "To improve my character today, I can _____."
9. Whatever you have listed above, go to work on that today!

GET YOUR OWN: A Lesson in Self-Sufficiency

8

"God bless the child that's got his own." ~ Billie Holiday, Singer

Wilma made a sweet potato soufflé to take to the office potluck dinner party. Everybody was bringing something and she could not wait to taste the delicious offerings that were about to grace her palette. She took a shower, put on something comfortable and cute, reapplied her makeup, ran her fingers through her bob, threw on her earrings, then headed out the door.

Sam was there and so was Reggie. These superstar brothers were invited from another floor in the building, and all the women were going to flock to them. To Wilma's surprise, Sam brought a 7-layer chocolate cake, her favorite, and Reggie brought a deep dish peach cobbler. These men weren't playing!

Everyone's dish looked mouth-watering, except Taylor's and Jordan's. These women didn't bring anything, at least nothing to eat. They came scantily clad in "club" attire showing all of their "assets." Sure, this was an after-hours party, but it was still a work function. Their outfits were totally unacceptable.

Taylor made a beeline toward Sam. Dang! He's never going to talk to Wilma with Taylor throwing it at him! Jordan mingled, and even Reggie got a chance to mingle, but Sam was hemmed up all night long and looked like he was enjoying himself with Taylor. He glanced at Wilma a few times during the night, but he continued to talk to Taylor and even accepted her phone number when the night was winding down.

Everyone made a plate to go, even Taylor and Jordan, and then said their goodnights. Wilma turned to leave when she felt a hand on her elbow. "You're not leaving without saying goodbye, are you?" It was Sam. Wilma said, "Oh. I thought you had left with Taylor." Sam responded, "Nah, I'd never leave with her. She didn't bring anything to the table."

Ladies, the moral of the story is, *you need to bring something to the table* (see Ecclesiastes 5:18-19). When a person has something of substance to offer someone else, that person has value and can add value to someone else's life. Be a woman of value. Be a woman that has more than a pretty face, a fabulous weave, and a nice pair of legs. As the Bible tells us, beauty is fleeting (Proverbs 31:30). So I ask, what else you got?

Here is a list of BASIC things a 21st century virtuous woman brings to the table:

Spiritual Order

- Daily prayer
- Bible study (self or group)
- Fellowship with other Christians
- Volunteer work
- Charity
- Meditation
- Quiet time

Health & Wellness Lifestyle

- No smoking

- No excessive drinking
- Regular dental check-ups
- Regular physical activity (i.e., sports, exercise, dance)
- Minimal junk food
- A diet with plenty of fruits and vegetables
- Plenty of rest and relaxation
- Annual gynecological check-ups including pap smear
- Plenty of water
- Annual well visits with your physician
- Healthy, supportive relationships
- Pampering time

Personal Presentation

- Daily showers/baths
- Flattering hairstyle
- Clean and well-kept fingernails and toenails
- Tasteful makeup (light layer of lip color will do)
- Well-coordinated, properly-fitted outfit for your size
- Proper dress for the occasion (never trashy or showing too much skin)
- Moisturized skin (please, ladies, no ash or crust!)
- Clean teeth, healthy smile
- Pleasant fragrance

Household Needs

- Home (own or lease)
- Reliable transportation
- Cooking
- Cleaning
- Decorating for personalization
- Laundry
- Grocery shopping

- Husband care (if you have a husband)
- Child care (if you have a child(ren))

Financial Order

- Checking and savings account
- Debt elimination plan
- Paying bills regularly and on time
- Legitimate and sufficient source of earned income
- Retirement plan
- "Play money" (money to spend on fun)
- Investments
- Good credit score

So, how do you measure up to the list? It wasn't necessarily in order of importance, so don't get caught up on that. And, some things may not apply to you, like the debt elimination plan if you don't have any debt. I must confess that I am working towards having and maintaining everything on this list. And, that's what I suggest for you. Know where you fall short, and work towards it. The more you can check off of this list and say, "I got that!" the more you got it going on! The more you "got it going on," the more you bring to the table. When you know what you bring to the table, when you know that you have lifted yourself up and aren't waiting for someone else to do it, you are "value-full." Then you can add to other people, instead of constantly taking from them.

A word of caution, "Do not think more highly of yourself than you ought, but rather think of yourself with sober judgment, in accordance with the measure of faith God has given you." – Romans 12:3. In other words, don't get "the big head" or conceited just because you have it going on. God has blessed you to have it in order to share it, not flaunt it.

Sidebar: At the same time, you are not blessed in order to enable some man that just wants to live off of you. A 21st century virtuous woman does not let deadbeats live off of her and suck her dry. This behavior does not fall under "volunteer and donate." Insist that any man that's with you also brings something to the table or send him on his way! Okay, I'm getting off my soapbox now.

[VIRTUOUS STEPS]

1. Go through the list and see how you measure up. What would you like to work on next? Decide and write it down. Now go for it!
2. Consider this: being a 21st century virtuous woman has nothing to do with how pretty you are; it has everything to do with who you are and what substantive value you add to your world.

BOLDLY GO WHERE NO WOMAN HAS GONE BEFORE:
A Lesson in Boldness

9

"Freedom lies in being bold."~ Robert Frost, American Poet

To be bold is to be daring and courageous, to bravely move forward, even when it seems risky to do so. Barack and Michelle Obama boldly went after the presidency. Oprah Winfrey boldly went after her career in journalism. Tyra Banks boldly went after her place in the fashion world. Susan L. Taylor boldly went for her Bachelor's degree in her adulthood. Vanessa L. Williams boldly went after the title of Miss America. Our ancestors boldly survived slavery to leave us a legacy of resilience that brings with it the knowledge that we can endure and become anything.

Sojourner Truth, Harriet Tubman, Rosa Parks, Coretta Scott King, Mary McCloud Bethune, and Maya Angelou and are just a few of the women who were bold enough to walk in their purpose. Where would we be if Sojourner Truth had not been bold enough to be the first black woman to speak out against slavery? Where would we be if Harriet Tubman had not been bold enough to lead the Underground Railroad? Where would we be if Rosa Parks had not been bold enough to refuse to move to the back of the bus that day? Where would we be if Coretta Scott King had not been bold enough to take a stance on skin complexion amongst black people, believing that it was not an indicator of a person's worth? Where would we be if Mary McCloud Bethune had not been bold enough to found a college for young black women and dedicate her life to the empowerment of black people? Where would we be if Maya Angelou had not been bold enough to teach, dance, sing, and write what was in her soul and change the world? Where would we be if the impact of the boldness of these brave women had not touched and changed our history?

You can find boldness everywhere you look: in the eyes of the mother who walks confidently to the counter to spend her last $10 on diapers, in the attitude of the speaker on stage who talks of losing a breast to cancer, in the heart of a daughter as she tells the doctor it is NOT her mother's time to die and just perform the operation, in the mind of the battered wife as she leaves her abusive husband for the last time, in the walk of the graduate as she marches past the professor that told her she would never graduate from "his" program. Boldness is everywhere! Is it in you?

You come from a long history of bold women and there continues to be bold women around you, in some way, every day. Becoming the virtuous woman you were meant to be requires you to embrace this boldness, to walk confidently, courageously, and daringly into the future that God has intended for you (see Psalm 138:3, Proverbs 28:1). Be bold enough to be the best you can be, in spite of family or friends that may want to hold you back. Be bold enough to not only say, "Yes, I can," but "YES, I AM."

[VIRTUOUS STEPS]

1. What is it that you know you must do, but you haven't done because you are afraid to do it? Write it down. Now write down the best and worst things that can happen if you do it. Now, consider if the best thing and the worst thing were to

actually happen. The best thing is pretty good, huh? And the worst thing may be pretty bad (or not), but, is it something that's in God's will? Is it something that will ultimately help you to grow into a virtuous woman? If so, confront your fears, be bold, and go for the gold! You CAN make a difference!

2. Write down all the women you can think of that you admire for their boldness. Consider how boldness adds to their personality and what they accomplished with their boldness. Now, write down your name with these same women. Consider how boldness will help you to become the woman you were created to be and do what you were created to do.

DON'T BE A DOORMAT: A Lesson in Setting Boundaries

10

"Boundaries are to protect life, not to limit pleasures."
~ Edwin Louis Cole, Minister

People who set boundaries for their relationships and do not compromise these boundaries, have a stronger sense of self-worth and contentment. Boundaries are rules that people must follow when dealing with you. Boundaries tell people how far they can go with you, what they can say to you, what they can do to you, and what they can expect from you.

Pamela was reared by her grandmother, who did not instill a strong sense of self-worth in her. Pamela only knew that she was to do what was asked of her, when it was asked. When she went off to college, she carried this mentality with her: that she needed to do what was asked of her. This love-starved girl became prey for the older college boys. Whenever they asked anything of her, whether it was money or sex, she gave it freely, because that was what was asked of her. She didn't know how to say no. Heck, she didn't even know that she should say no. She had no sense of self-worth and had set no boundaries for herself.

Pamela became friends with Danielle, who ended up being a blessing for her. Danielle was a Christian girl who took misguided

Pamela under her wing. Danielle taught Pamela all about self-worth, self-respect, and self-love. She taught her about setting boundaries so that others would respect her and value her or leave her alone. She taught her that she did not have to be used or compromise herself or her body.

For the first time in her life, Pamela felt like *somebody*. She said "no" a lot more frequently. She had real friends instead of a bunch of users. She valued herself and her friends also valued her. She even had a boyfriend now who knew how to treat her well and with respect. He "tried" her a few times as most men will just to see what they can get away with. But Pamela held her own. Her boyfriend learned that he could not curse her, he could not yell at her, he could not demand anything of her, and he could not call her all hours of the night. She stood her ground with him. So if he wanted to talk to her or spend time with her, he had to do it her way or not at all. He had to speak nicely and call her during waking hours. No, she didn't allow herself to be a booty call. Once he was allowed to spend quality time with her and get to know her, he saw that he really liked Pamela and wanted to be more than her friend. This is how Pamela got herself a man! And more importantly, this is how she found herself; by honoring herself and being true to herself.

Boundaries should be set for all of your relationships: work, friendships, casual, romantic, family, and marital. People will do to you only what you allow them to do to you. Learn to honor yourself and God in you. Here are some boundaries that virtuous women have. Feel free to add your own.

1. Don't allow people to curse/cuss you.
2. Don't allow people to physically abuse you. (Don't let anyone hit or push you.)
3. Don't allow people to emotionally abuse you. (Don't let anyone talk badly to you, i.e., "put you down.")

4. Don't allow people to financially take advantage of you. (Don't lend/give money to "friends" or men who supposedly "like" or "love" you. Make good financial decisions for yourself. Give it only if you have it to give and don't really need it anyway, and only to someone who truly cares about you.)
5. Don't allow people to use you sexually. (Hint: In cases of random, casual sex…you're being used for sure.)
6. Don't allow men you are not dating exclusively to call you after an acceptable hour. (In most cases, this should probably not be after 11 pm.)
7. Don't be a booty call. Period.

If someone does not respect your boundaries, what should you do? Leave them alone and/or limit your contact with them. People who won't respect your boundaries do not deserve a place up front and center in your life. Many people become enraged when their boundaries are crossed. They become violent because they were "disrespected." This is no reason to argue, fight, slash tires, throw rocks through windows, or shoot someone. Simply cease the communication and walk away. Walk away from the person. Walk away from the relationship…permanently, if either your desire or the situation calls for it. Remember, a virtuous woman is a doormat for no one and must insist that her boundaries be respected. She is a child of the Living God and must be treated as such.

[VIRTUOUS STEPS]

1. Write out a list of boundaries you want to set for yourself.
2. Which ways have you repeatedly allowed people to dishonor you and in what situations?

3. Which people in your life do you feel do not honor your personal boundaries? Why do you think they do not honor your boundaries? Do you allow it?
4. What can you do differently to set boundaries for yourself and not compromise them?
5. Do you respect the boundaries that are set by other people? Why or why not?

TALKING THE TALK AND WALKING THE WALK:
A Lesson in Integrity

11

"Your life may be the only Bible some people read." ~Anonymous

When a woman does what she says, when her actions are consistent with her speech, when you can count on her, rely on her, and depend on her, then this person can be said to have integrity.

Having integrity implies a certain amount of inner peace. A person with integrity does not have conflict within herself regarding her own value and belief systems. Her words, thoughts, intentions, and actions are congruent. She stands for what she believes.

Furthermore, a virtuous woman does not let circumstances dictate her level of integrity. She does not play "tit for tat" and she does not "get even." She holds steadfast to her beliefs and values, even when the world around her is doing something different. Her words, actions, and behavior are consistent with what she believes, no matter what.

Dawn is a vibrant, earthy woman who just found out the hard way that her husband is cheating on her. She's hurt, enraged, and devastated—her whole world had just been turned upside down. Her first reaction is to go to one of her ex-boyfriends to have sex with him. She thinks of making that phone call, then imagines what her time with her ex would be like. She's crying so hard and she can't even make the phone call to him. Going for an extremely long walk helps. Going to the gym and attacking the punching bag helps, too. By this time, Dawn has released some of her emotions, but of course not enough. She calls that ex on her cell from the car. She goes home, takes a quick shower, smooths her hair, puts on some natural oils, then heads his way.

On the way there, Dawn has time to think. "Two wrongs, don't make a right," she hears her grandmother say. Then she starts talking to herself, "I thought you said cheating was wrong? Then what are you doing? Just where do you think you're going? Yeah, he screwed up, but do you have to be wrong, too?" Then Dawn started thinking about the can of worms she was about to open. If she had sex with her ex, he may not leave her alone. Who has he been with? What if she got a disease? What if she got pregnant? What if she and her husband worked it out? Could she live with being a cheater? That's the big question: "COULD I LIVE WITH BEING A CHEATER? WILL I BE ABLE TO STAND MYSELF IN THE MORNING? This goes against everything I believe in."

Dawn musters the good sense and strength to turn the car around. She goes to her best friend's house instead. She sends her ex a text message simply saying that she changed her mind and thanks anyway. After telling her best friend what happened (she had to talk to someone), her friend confirms that she did the right thing in cancelling her rendezvous. Her friend tells her that she would have regretted it in more ways than one, and reminds her how much she despises cheating. Her friend prays with her and they listen to music appropriate to the occasion over a bottle of wine. Dawn comes to realize how much she treasures her best friend, and how glad she is that she held true to her values and beliefs. She knew she would not have been able to live with herself otherwise. Dawn knows that she has a long road ahead of her. But, at least now she can go to God in prayer, with a clean conscience, giving thanks for her friend and for His comfort, and asking for His direction.

[VIRTUOUS STEPS]

1. In what area do you need to work on your integrity? In your finances? Your marriage? Your job? Your friendships? With yourself? How can you improve that today?

2. Think of one thing that you believe strongly in. Think of how you would feel if someone violated that belief, i.e., they acted in some way that went against your belief. How would that feel? What would you think? Now, consider if that someone was you? Is there something you have "preached" about that you haven't practiced? Get real with yourself today. If you have not practiced integrity, either start now practicing what you preach, or just quit preaching.

3. Does your life reflect what you say you believe in? For example, if you say that you believe in honoring your father and your mother, then consider the last time you spoke with them or checked on them. If you preach about the sanctity of marriage, then consider whether you have been totally faithful. If you preach about charity work, then consider the last time you donated your time or money to a charitable cause. If you have been low on integrity, get real with yourself, forgive yourself, and start now to demonstrate a higher level of integrity than ever before. "The man of integrity walks securely, but he who takes crooked paths will be found out." –Proverbs 10:9

IT'S TIME TO FORGIVE
(BUT YOU DON'T HAVE TO FORGET,
JUST DON'T RELIVE IT):
A Lesson in Forgiveness

12

"Forgive, and you will be forgiven." ~ Luke 6:37, *Holy Bible*

Many of us have some pretty big events, people, issues, etc. to forgive. These hurtful events/people may have shaped who we have become today; events like childhood abuse, molestation, rape, incest, infidelity, betrayal of confidence, emotional abuse, mental abuse, physical abuse, abandonment by a parent, childhood neglect, etc. Nowadays, you would be hard pressed to come across someone who has not had her own cross to bear. However through it all, we are still here. Now it's time to do the hard work. Now it's time to forgive and move on.

I know, it's easier said than done. However, consider what carrying that baggage does to you. It robs you of your happiness. How? By occupying space in your heart and mind where happiness can be instead. See, when you hold on to a negative event, you are in effect, not forgiving. When you relive the event, and feel the pain or anger you felt when the event occurred, you are not forgiving. When you are not forgiving, you are holding yourself hostage. Let me say that again. *When you are not forgiving, you are holding yourself hostage.* You are holding yourself hostage, waiting for a ransom that can never be paid.

When someone is taken hostage, usually there is a ransom, a sum of money that is demanded in exchange for the return of the loved one. Pay the money, get the loved one back. In the case of unforgivingness, your happiness is held hostage, in exchange for some sort of undoing of the past. Maybe the "injured" person wants the event to go away and to cease existing, even in her past. Or, maybe the "injured" person wants an apology or some sort of restitution from the offender. In any case, there is no repayment that can be collected to make the pain and/or anger go away and restore the "injured" person.

Let's look at what Eunice went through. Eunice loved her daddy dearly. One time when she was sick he brought her crayons and a coloring book. Another day he picked her up, bought her a tennis racket, and took her to play tennis for the first and last time. Eunice didn't spend that much time with her daddy, but she loved him anyway. One day, her mother, her mother's boyfriend, and her daddy all met with her in her pretty purple bedroom. Her daddy picked her up, sat her on his lap, and told her, "I'm not going to see you for a long time. Now go to your mommy." Then he handed Eunice over to her mother and was gone for good. Eunice was traumatized at just eight years old.

When Eunice became a young adult, she began to treat men poorly. Ultimately, she would end the relationship prematurely and without emotion. She had developed a fear of abandonment. Eunice eventually understood what was happening to her. She eventually understood that she was afraid that men would leave her. Worse than that, she was afraid that somehow she was unworthy, not good enough to have a man love her. When she realized this fear and why she felt this way, she despised her father for doing this to her. He was the first one to leave her. He was the first one to just give her away.

Eunice carried this fear and anger with her for decades, which became worse each time she found her father and he rejected her. She eventually worked with a therapist for a while, but the memory was too painful for her to continue. Later, she committed to doing the work on herself for her own healing. By reading self-help books, the *Holy Bible*, and praying, she discovered that forgiveness would free her. She saw her father as what he was: human. He was human with all the imperfections that humans have. He was only a product of his own life's experiences. He did only what he knew to do. Through prayer, she was reminded that she was not perfect and she too, in some way, had sinned against someone else. She learned that with God, sin is sin and there are no varying degrees of sin with God. To Him, each sin is just as bad as the next. So, she committed herself to forgiving her father, the man who initially introduced the feelings of fear and worthlessness into her life. Over time, Eunice did learn to forgive her father, just as her Heavenly Father has forgiven her.

Now, Eunice has somewhat of a friendship with her father. Ironically, he found her and conveyed his desire to establish a father-daughter relationship with her. Although Eunice has forgiven her father, she no longer needs or desires that kind of relationship with him. She has truly moved on. She only wants to be friends.

Today, Eunice is closer to true happiness than she has ever been because she chose to forgive. Who or what will you forgive today?

[VIRTUOUS STEPS]

1. First, recognize the anger, the pain. Where did it come from? Purge yourself (get alone and cry, scream, yell, fuss, hit pillows, punch a punching bag, etc.) of the anger and the pain. Then, CHOOSE to forgive. Yes, in some cases it will be extremely challenging. But you're up for the challenge! We're talking about your life TODAY. It's time to free the hostage! It's time to free yourself. It's all about

YOU. Leave the past in the past. Don't bring it into today or take it into tomorrow. Take back your life and begin to claim your happiness today. Choose to forgive.

2. Second, look for the learning experience. Look for the blessing. How were you made stronger and wiser because of what you went through? How can you become a better person because of it? Turn that negative into a positive. Move on.

3. Third, consider how you are able to help someone because of what you went through. Let God use you for His Glory. You ARE stronger. You ARE wiser. You can do it. Go bless someone.

4. Fourth, breathe. You're fine. You have survived; now it's time to thrive!

(By the way, if you are the person that you need to forgive, go easy on yourself. We all make mistakes, no matter how big or small. Be woman enough to own your mistakes. Admit it, accept any reasonable backlash from it, correct the mistake if you can, learn from it, forgive yourself for it, grow because of it, and move on! You've got God's work to do.)

REVENGE—A DISH BEST LEFT UNSERVED:
A Lesson in Getting Revenge

13

"In taking revenge, a man is but even with his enemy; but in passing it over, he is superior."

~ Francis Bacon, English Philosopher

Sometimes, when we are offended and/or hurt, we want to "get back at" the offender. We want to make this person "pay." We want to "show them." Sometimes, "teaching him a lesson" sounds mighty good and seems, at the time, like it might feel mighty good, too. However, retaliation isn't in God's will for His children. Of all the things we are to take care of, exacting revenge isn't one of them.

Collette is a lovely young Christian woman. She's a devoted wife, wonderful mother, caring daughter, and loyal friend. She recently, however, felt betrayed by her husband Leon. She felt he had total disrespect and disregard for her feelings. His daughter (from a previous relationship) was getting married, and she, his wife, was not invited to the wedding. Leon elected to go to the wedding without her, in honor of his daughter's wishes and dishonoring Collette as his wife. He elected to partake of the festivities with his daughter and her mother, neither of which particularly cared for Collette. See, this wasn't the first time Collette felt Leon totally disrespected her with his daughter and his daughter's mother and she was fed up. At first, Collette was going to divorce him. Oh, yes, she was quite pissed and this was the last straw. But after calming down, she realized that she was going to make him pay.

But, the more Collette thought about "making him sorry", the more she realized that her plot for revenge was turning her into someone she didn't want to be. She could feel herself becoming evil and vindictive. Her temperature was going up and probably her blood pressure, too. She was so angry she couldn't see straight. Collette became cynical, sarcastic, and couldn't focus on the things that made her happy because her anger kept getting in the way. And for what? Because her husband was a fool behind his daughter and her mother? *No one and no amount of anger is worth you losing yourself over.* And by the way, Collette had some ideas up her sleeve besides the divorce. Heck, the divorce would have let him off too easy.

So, instead, Collette, being a Christian woman, sought God's word on the subject of revenge. After all, who could do a better job of exacting justice on her behalf: her or God?

"You shall not take revenge or bear any grudge against the sons of your people, but you shall love your neighbor as yourself. I am the Lord." Leviticus 19:18. "Dearly beloved, avenge not yourselves, but rather give place unto wrath: for it is written, Vengeance is mine; I will repay, saith the Lord." Romans 12:19. God commands us not to take revenge against anyone. He states in the Bible that He will take care of it; that He will make it right. We just have to wait. God does everything in His perfect time and in His perfect way. In the meantime, we are to continue to live within His will, with a clean heart and with pure thoughts.

Pure thoughts? Yes, pure thoughts, thoughts that you wouldn't mind sharing with God. If you "let it go" but still think about sticking a dagger through her eye, pouring sugar in his tank, or a plethora of ways to make your offender black and blue, then you are poisoning your own mind and driving yourself crazy.

I imagine that certainly one of the reasons that the Lord wants us to leave vengeance up to Him is because it is a waste of time for us. We always say that "life is too short." If we can literally figure out how much time we might have on this earth then compare that to how much time God has, it makes sense that He should handle it since He clearly has the time. Our time is precious and short, and once spent, we cannot get it back.

Another reason we are to leave vengeance to our Father, I believe, is because He says vengeance is His. If God says something is His, who are we to *try* to take it away from Him? In trying to avenge ourselves (or someone else), God may elect not to since clearly we would think that we could do a better job of it than He could. How absurd does that sound?

Yet another reason that we should leave vengeance to God is that He is the Judge, not us. Think of a courtroom. There's the offender's side (the defendant) and the offendee's side (the prosecutor). God *knows* both sides of the situation. He knows if the situation is not as bad as we think, as bad as we think, or worse than we think, and He will Judge according to what He knows (and remember, He knows all).

Besides, remember the saying, "What goes around comes around?" And, "You reap what you sow?" And do your remember the Law of Cause and Effect? Basically, when we think about it, we realize it's already taken care of, it's already done, and all we need to do is forgive and move on from offense and/or hurt feelings.

Our job, when we are hurt and/or offended, *is* to forgive and move on from the offense and/or hurt feelings. We are to nourish our soul and our spirit. We are to honor God and ourselves by taking care of ourselves. We are to pray and meditate. We are to fast, if needed. We must learn and grow from the experience, just as we must learn and grow from all of our experiences.

[VIRTUOUS STEPS]

1. **What offense or hurt feelings are you holding onto?** *Realize now that these feelings keep you trapped in the moment of offense and are stealing your time and your joy.*

2. **Pray for your offender and speak well of your offender, or don't speak of him/her at all.** Collette dropped the whole incident with Leon, refusing to talk about it anymore because it was done and over. She did not want to be trapped in the moment of the offense and give it power over her present or future. Collette chose to remove his daughter and her mother as the topic of unnecessary discussion. Whatever they had against her, she decided to let it be their problem and not hers. This freed her to move forward in her life and focus on doing God's will in her life and in her marriage with Leon. She prayed for all of them, then "left it at the altar."

3. **Be good to your offender.** *This helps you* to grow in love. To do the "Christianly thing," Collette bought her husband's daughter a wedding gift and sent him off with kisses. Here are a couple of scriptures that helped Collette get to the point to where she could give the wedding gift and begin to repair her relationship with her husband: a) "Therefore if thine enemy hunger, feed him; if he thirst, give him drink: for in so doing thou shalt heap coals of fire on his head." Romans 12:20. b) "Love is patient, love is kind. It does not envy, it does not boast, it is not proud. It is not rude, it is not self-seeking, it is not easily angered, it keeps no record of wrongs. Love does not

delight in evil but rejoices with the truth. It always protects, always trusts, always hopes always perseveres. Love never fails….." 1 Corinthians 13 4-8.

4. **Think (meditate) on good things**. Don't keep reliving the offense over and over in your head. When you find yourself thinking about happened, about how bad he, she, or they hurt you or stabbed you in the back, force yourself to think about something good and productive in your life. In this way, you will start to move away from the bad experience and begin to grow.

5. **Pray for yourself**. Pray for a right mind, a clean heart, a healed soul, a growing spirit, and a fresh perspective. Give thanks for surviving the offense/hurt feeling and for the ability to move on.

YOU'RE GONNA GET IT:
A Lesson in Sowing and Reaping

14

"…for whatever a man sows, that he will also reap."
~ Galatians 6:7, *Holy Bible*

Sowing and reaping is a very simple concept that I think we often fail to apply to our lives. Let me give an example of this basic concept. Start with a desire to grow an apple tree. From that desire, you must make a decision to do whatever it takes to grow that apple tree. First, you acquire the basic things you need to plant this tree: apple seeds, tools for planting, fertilizer, etc. Next, you till the ground before planting the seeds. With water and sunlight, your tree will grow. You guard your tree against weeds, stray dogs, and anything else that would threaten the growth of your apple tree. You remain steadfast to the vision of your tree, and one day you are pleased when the apple tree is full grown and bears beautiful, delicious, juicy red apples.

Now, let's apply this concept. Stacie needs to relax and have some fun. She has worked nine months straight, without any vacation time. She's starting to feel burnout. She has a *desire* to get away. While flipping through a travel magazine, she sees how perfectly beautiful Turk & Caicos is and *decides* that will be where she travels. To maximize her vacation (and her safety), Stacie decides to invite four of her closest friends and gives herself and her friends six months to prepare for their vacation. During the six months, Stacie arranges for someone to cover for her on her job for the week she will be gone and puts in for her PTO (paid time off). She pays for her vacation in three months, then continues to save for spending money and incidentals.

All of her friends follow this plan and they have a great time vacationing in Turks & Caicos except one friend. Jaz, procrastinated with her saving and her vacation pay plan and therefore was unable to go. Stacie and all of her friends, including Jaz, reaped what they sowed. Stacie and three of her friends prepared or *sowed* for a great vacation. And a great vacation is what they reaped. Jaz, on the other hand, inevitably prepared to remain home. She spent money the way she always did, let the deadline for final payment of the trip pass, and did not request time off. ("If you always do, what you've always done, you'll get what you've always gotten." –Anthony Robbins)

So this is what Jaz sowed, and what she reaped was a week of wondering how much fun her friends were having without her while she stayed behind and worked. Jaz wanted to go, but she failed to prepare; she failed to sow. Just as you can't have an apple tree without planting apple seeds, Jaz couldn't go on vacation without proper preparation. *Wanting* something is not the same thing as *working* for something. Wanting something is only the first step. If your desire is strong enough, then you must plan for success. You must prepare for success. You must prepare and expect favorable results.

I mentioned before that God does not give you more than you can handle. This doesn't just apply to trials and tribulations. It also applies to blessings and miracles. For example, if you ultimately want seven children, but you can't or don't handle or care for the two children that you have, then don't be surprised if you don't get your seven children. Or, if you want a promotion on your job, but are late going to work every day, take long lunch breaks, miss deadlines, and have a bad attitude, you probably won't be blessed with that promotion.

Similarly, if you need a new car, but the inside of your current car hasn't been cleaned out in six months and the outside hasn't been washed in three months, then you are not being a good steward of the car you have, so why should you be blessed with another? You have to take care of what you have and make room for what you want. Do you understand what I'm saying? You cannot reap what you don't sow. Life just doesn't work like that.

So, *decide* which apples you want out of life. Go *plant* those apple seeds. *Watch* over what you have planted. *Prepare* for a big apple tree. *Expect* to enjoy those beautiful, delicious, juicy apples and *patiently wait* for your abundance to happen.

[VIRTUOUS STEPS]

1. What is it that you really want right now? A career change, new car, dream home, well-mannered children, the perfect wedding gown, what? Get crystal clear about what you want. Write it down. What seeds do you need to plant, that is, what do you need to do to prepare for what you want? What is your plan? Write it down.
2. Now that you have a plan, commit to specific action! The best plan will not yield results without targeted action. Remember that!
3. What counterproductive behavior has been yielding bad fruit? If you don't know, look at the fruit you have yielded. Now work backwards to figure out the counterproductive behavior that produced the bad fruit. Commit to changing that behavior in order to yield better fruit. Cause and effect, baby, cause and effect.

DO THE RIGHT THANG: A Lesson in Doing What's Right (Even When You Don't Feel Like It)

15

"The wrong thing done for the right reason is still the wrong thing."
~Unknown

Shelby is a beautiful, vibrant 35 year-old, executive at a major bank. She has loyal friends, gorgeous children, lives in an affluent neighborhood and has a luxury ride. And get this: her husband, Anthony, is tall, dark, and handsome. He's an attorney at a top law firm, has an awesome body, is a great father, and a good son. From the outside looking in, Shelby has all she has ever wanted.

But, Shelby is love starved. She feels she does all the right things, but she still does not get the attention and affection from her husband that she craves. They have good sex often enough, but outside of the bedroom, he barely touches her. And if they get into a silly argument, he definitely doesn't touch her. Months go by and she begins to wonder whether he still finds her attractive since he never says, "Baby, you're beautiful." Sometimes she even wonders if he still loves her because the hand-holding, bear hugs, and forehead kisses have stopped. She feels that she can't live like this!

Here comes Tyree. Tyree is a fine specimen! He's strong, powerful, smells wonderful (that is her weakness), and she noticed he had a nice, melodic baritone voice when he said, "It's a pleasure meeting you, Miss Shelby." What? And manners, too? He asked if he could call her, about banking issues of course, and she gave her permission. Shelby and Tyree's conversation strayed from banking to bowling and everything in between. She hadn't felt that listened to in a long time. She felt like she was really connecting with him. And when Tyree told her he would love to run his fingers through her hair, grab her by the back of the head and... she felt a little light-headed. What was the rest of what he said?

At this point, Shelby knows that this relationship with Tyree is going too far. But she feels so alive. Her husband Anthony isn't paying her any attention anyway and this new man, well, he's taking up the slack. She deserves to feel this good every day, doesn't she? She deserves to be told that she's fine, doesn't she? She deserves to be wined and dined, right? And she's a good wife, doing all the cooking, cleaning, and working outside the home, listening to Anthony's complaints about work, laughing at his stupid jokes, not complaining when he hangs out with the fellas, yada yada yada. The last time Anthony gazed deeply into her eyes was...when? Yeah, she needs this, and what Anthony doesn't know won't hurt him, right?

Are you kidding me? Don't get me wrong. Being a woman myself, I completely understand how Shelby feels. Completely. And she absolutely deserves to have the attention and affection that she craves. She deserves to have the attention and affection that she craves FROM HER HUSBAND. Ladies, *the wrong thing done for the right reason is still the wrong thing.* Don't get it twisted. No matter if it's cheating, telling a little "white lie," taking office supplies from work for your personal use (yeah, yeah, I know), borrowing your friend's car without asking—whatever.. It's still wrong and there is no way to justify wrong. Being human, we may understand it, but it's still WRONG (see James 4:17).

Shelby is clearly doing the wrong thing for the right reason (to get attention and affection that is making her feel amazing), but it's still the wrong thing because the attention and affection is not coming from her husband, since she is after all, a married woman...remember that?

So, why is it wrong, you ask? Because she's married! She entered into an agreement with this man and with God to do right by this man, no matter what. Marriage is a sacred vow, a covenant. These particular promises are to be taken very seriously because the vows don't just involve you, they involve God. So, Shelby isn't just cheating on her husband (and although she hasn't had sex with Tyree yet, she's still cheating because she is having a romantic relationship with him), she's cheating herself and cheating on God, since He is supposed to be a part of the marriage as well.

What's the right thing for Shelby to do? She needs to end it immediately with Tyree. Then she needs to sit down with her husband and tell him how she feels, what she needs, and then begin to show him daily how to give her what she needs. It may take time. She's got to be patient. But since Anthony is a good, God-fearing man who truly does love her, he will put forth the effort to please her. Re-igniting the romance in their lives is what's needed. And she can take inventory of his feelings as well, and see exactly how satisfied he is with their relationship. Maybe there is something else he needs from her that will help him give her what she needs. And above all else, Shelby's got to pray and meditate on it. She's got to learn to wait on the Lord.

God would never have us do the wrong thing for the right reason. That is NOT His will. I caution you to think before you act. Strongly consider the long term consequences of your actions.

[VIRTUOUS STEPS]

1. List three times when you did the wrong thing for the right reason. It doesn't have to involve cheating, like in Shelby's situation. Was there anything else you could have done? If you didn't see another way more in line with God's will, could you have trusted and waited on God?

2. Meditate on this: God will not give you more than you can handle (1 Corinthians 10:13).

3. If you are currently in a situation where you are contemplating doing something wrong, reflect on the lesson to be learned before you act on a bad decision. Are you avoiding doing the right thing because it makes you uncomfortable? What are the long term repercussions for doing the wrong thing? Do you want to do the right thing, but it will cause you pain or grief if you do? Will you be ostracized by your family or friends if you do the right thing? Are you relying on your own strength instead of God's insight and perfect will? Name what you need and claim it as your own! Being a child of God, anything you want that's within His will He will provide. Wait on the Lord.

(By the way, the characters above are fictitious, so if I stepped on any toes, check yourself!)

DON'T TAKE ANYTHING FOR GRANTED:
(better yet, don't complain)
A Lesson in Gratitude

16

"Gratitude is not only the greatest of virtues, but the parent of all the others."
~ Marcus Tullio Cicero, Roman Philosopher

Let me guess: You got up today, brushed your teeth, perhaps grabbed a bite to eat, then hurried out the door. You went through your entire day, possibly avoided an argument, or even an accident, then made it home safely. You grabbed another bite to eat, then went to bed. Next day: Same thing. At what point do we stop to think or meditate on all of the blessings bestowed upon us directly from God or from God through other people? We still have our able bodies, our minds, valued relationships, clothes, food, shelter, air, freedom, and even some perks like television or transportation. So, when was the last time you said "thank you" and showed appreciation for all that you are and all that you have? When was the last time you said, "Thank you, Lord," and meant it? When was the last time you told someone "thank you" or showed someone appreciation?

Every day is a day to give thanks (see 1 Timothy 4:4). Why? Because every day is a gift from God; an opportunity to do it right, an opportunity to do more, an opportunity to do it better. Every day is a day to show God that our faith is in Him, that we trust Him to lead us, guide us, and show us His perfect will on our lives. Each day is a day to show Him that we love Him (see 1 Chronicles 16:8). Each day is a day to show Him how we will use what He has given us to fulfill His purpose. And, let's face it: We could be a lot worse off, now couldn't we?

Halley is an average woman, except for one thing: She's got Jesus. She looks average, talks average, walks average…she's just average. To look at her, you may think there was nothing spectacular about her. Then she got laid off from her job. You know what she said? "Thank you, Jesus! I didn't like that job anyway!" Then, her car broke down and she didn't have the money to get it fixed. You know what she said? "Thank you, Jesus! I need to walk for exercise anyway!" Then her best friends moved away. She said, "Thank you, Lord! Maybe I can save some money now since I won't be eating out all the time!"

Months went by. Halley was still collecting unemployment checks. She was without her close friends and couldn't get around since her car still had not been fixed. Each day, she remained faithful and continued to thank God. Halley realized she STILL had it good. She still had the basics and she knew that God would provide. She knew that He doesn't always come when you want Him, but He's always right on time! She never complained. She knew God didn't want to hear that mess. But, she did begin to pray more fervently.

She prayed for the job that God had for her. She prayed for a new car (Forget the old one. She may as well pray for what she wanted!). She prayed for her friends' health and happiness. She prayed to make new Christian friends so that she would have someone to hang out with. She continued to fellowship with other Christians and continued to pay her tithes. She volunteered with organizations in her community working with the elderly.

A couple of months later, her prayers were answered. One person she met while doing volunteer work recommended her for a job. Halley got that job and it paid $20,000 more per year than her last job! She was able to work from home on most days, which made her happy. With the pay increase, she was able to buy the car she wanted. And since she was making more money, she organized a trip with her new friends and her old friends to go on a cruise to the South Caribbean. While on her vacation, her friends talked about how good she looked since she had toned up from all that walking when she didn't have a car!

Halley had always remained positive and grateful for what she did have, even when it seemed like things just weren't going her way. She knew that complaining blocks blessings. She knew that being ungrateful blocks blessings. She knew that having an "attitude of gratitude" is best for her spirit and shows God that she appreciates Him and all the ways He moves mysteriously in her life.

So, ladies, no complaining about what you do have, what you don't have, yo' baby daddy not paying child support, your broke down car, your tired feet working your tired job, your weight, no time, no money, and no man! (see Philippians 2:14) Forget the baby daddy and be grateful for the baby! Never mind that the car is broken. Be glad that you have a car that can get fixed! Be glad you have feet that can get tired and be glad that you have a job! If you don't like your job, don't complain about it. Just do the best you can while you're looking for another one! As for your weight, be thankful you are being real about it and that you have seen yet another day where you can make a change. If you don't have enough time or money, figure out a plan to where you have more and be appreciative of the fact that you can co-create your future with the Ultimate Creator in order to live life more abundantly! Maybe that new business you wanted to start is waiting for you! As for the man…well, that's another chapter. But, suffice it to say, be grateful you have this time alone to get yourself right. This is your time to drop the baggage. This is your time to deal with your issues. This is your time to get yourself right before your Mr. Right. Rejoice! It would be a shame for him to come now, and you're not ready for him! So, thank God that He is holding onto your man for you until you're ready!

[VIRTUOUS STEPS]

1. Call someone today to say "thank you."
2. Buy a pack of thank you cards and send out the whole pack to people you really appreciate.
3. Offer to do something for someone who has done something for you.
4. Commit a random act of kindness to show gratitude to your Heavenly Father.
5. When someone does something nice for you, no matter how big or small the act, show your appreciation. At the very least, say "thank you." For example, if someone lets you cut in front of them while driving, wave at them to say "thank you." If a man holds the door open for you, say "thank you" and smile. If your nail technician does a great job on your nails, give her at least a 15% tip to show your gratitude. (That's right…tip her!) If you have been blessed by an older woman, take her out to lunch. If your best friend has a birthday coming up, bake her a cake. Show gratitude, girl!
6. Before you go to bed, thank God for all that you have and all that you are. Vow to live a life of gratitude. Then, when you awake the next morning, thank God for letting you see another day (1 Chronicles 23:30).

WHAT HAVE YOU DONE FOR SOMEONE LATELY:
A Lesson in Helping the Less Fortunate

17

"We make a living by what we get, but we make a life
by what we give."
~ Winston Churchill, Nobel Prize Recipient

When was the last time you helped someone else? I don't mean that you gave a homeless person a dollar (which is good, by the way), I mean REALLY helped someone? Giving a homeless person a dollar is good for a minute, but what have you done that could help someone for a lifetime? Some examples are providing Thanksgiving Dinner for a family, spending time at the orphanage monthly, donating your professional services to some organization on a regular basis, giving clothes and other necessities to the Women's Shelter as often as possible, etc.

Pilar is a speech therapist. Every year for a few weeks she travels abroad to give free speech therapy services to children who have cleft lips and/or palate. She teaches these children to speak and to eat after they have had surgery to repair their deformities. Pilar feels good when she had helped children who otherwise would have not had speech therapy had it not been for her and the organization she works with.

Ruth is a belly dancer. When women learn of her skill, they become intrigued. Ruth began to notice that more and more older married women spoke of wanting to put the spice back in their marriages, so Ruth began to teach belly dancing at the local recreation center one night per month at no charge, specifically for those women who want to enliven their marriages. Ruth is tickled every time she hears one of her students stories of how her husband looks at her in a different way, or how another's husband buys her gifts, or how another's husband takes her on romantic trips now, or how yet another's husband actually remembered to celebrate their anniversary.

Pat is a manicurist. Every three months she goes to the Women's Shelter to give free manicures and pedicures and free classes on nail care to the women who have upcoming job interviews. She is excited when the women appreciate her work. Whenever she returns, she's pleased to notice that some women have moved on, have gotten jobs, and are doing quite well. She hopes the same for all of them.

Zoe was a teen mom. She had a really hard time rearing her child alone. Because of the trying times she went through, Zoe speaks to young girls all across the country to tell her story of the impact motherhood had on her life at such an early age, how she could have done things differently, and how they can choose to design their lives right now in order to give themselves the best future.

Gayle is a busy college student. She comes from a huge, loving family. She learned from one of the charitable organizations in her community that there were little girls who needed good female role models in their lives, someone who would spend time with them, and value them. Gayle became a "big sister" to a little girl whose mother had died in a car accident. She made time for the little girl, having sleepovers, going on shopping sprees, helping her select feminine products, taking her to family functions, and helping her with schoolwork, making a difference.

All of these women are making a difference. They are making a difference not only in the lives of others, but in their own lives. While they are helping to change a potentially negative outcome in someone's life, they are also enriching their own (see Philippians 2:4).

Give what you want to have (2 Corinthians 9:6). If you want someone to help you in your time of need, then help someone in her time of need. If you want more money, then give money. If you want more clothes, then give your clothes. If you want more love, then give love away. Let God lead you in committing your acts of charity. He has blessed you in ways you may or may not realize right now. You have something that you can share with someone else. When you hold onto something so tightly that you refuse to give away because you are afraid that there won't be enough for you, you're right. You have to get to a place within yourself where you can trust that God will provide for all of your needs. You demonstrate this trust in God by letting go of what you have in order to bless someone else. Go about doing God's work and He will repay you for it (Proverbs 19:17). God loves a cheerful giver, so whatever you give, be glad to give it. Whether it's time, money, material things, or expertise, give it cheerfully as giving unto the Lord (2 Corinthians 9:7).

[VIRTUOUS STEPS]

1. What can you give cheerfully? Your time? Money? Clothes? Children's toys? Old computers? Shoes? Your expertise? Don't be stingy! Make a list of whatever you can cheerfully give this week, this month, or this year. Give it then watch how God works!

2. Think of a time when someone did something to help you. Did you appreciate it? Did they do it willfully or begrudgingly? How did the spirit in which they gave make you feel? Consider your own attitude the next time you decide to do something for someone else. If you don't do it with the right attitude, in the right spirit, it still won't please God. So, if you do it, get your heart right, and make it count!

IT'S NOT ABOUT YOU:
A Lesson in Thinking Beyond Yourself

18

"No one can find inner peace except by working, not in a self-
centered way,
but for the whole human family."
~ Peace Pilgrim, Peace Activist

Caitlyn works at a busy daycare with a bunch of rowdy kids. She feels she has outgrown this job and has frequently prayed for another one, one more suited to her qualifications and temperament. See, Caitlyn graduated from college recently, earning her Bachelor's degree in Education. She wants to teach elementary school children now, in a little school just outside the city where life is slower and quieter.

Today is particularly rough on Caitlyn. Her cranky boss is on the warpath and is yelling at everyone, and Caitlyn is no exception. When her boss approached her, cussing and yelling about things out of Caitlyn's control, Caitlyn started cussing and yelling back—she can give it to the best of them. Although this behavior is not Caitlyn's style, when she is pushed too far, the world sees the very worst of her.

Because of Caitlyn's "insubordination," she gets suspended from her job. She is still cussing and fussing as she's walking out. On her way home, she calls her mother to tell her what happened. Her mother explains to her, "Baby, that woman already had problems. She wasn't really attacking you personally, she was just frustrated with her world. When you went on the defensive and fussed back, you made her problem about YOU, and then it WAS your problem. Baby, *it wasn't about YOU.*"

How many times have we had someone act crazy towards us and we lashed back? Dozens of times! We REACT so much and become defensive so often it's a habit. The wise people know that these outbursts that people have toward us is not about us. It's all about them and the rotten day, or worse yet, the rotten life, they are having. Choose not to be a part of the rottenness.

To some degree, having someone yelling at you or treating you badly may hurt your feelings. But remember, hurt people hurt people. Choose not to take what is said to heart. Recognize that the angry, hurtful person is choosing a non-constructive, inconsiderate way of dealing with her negative emotions and instead of attacking her problem, she chooses to attack other people.

No, you absolutely must not let anyone abuse you, verbally or otherwise. I do not condone that. What I am suggesting is finding a way to appropriately deal with them in the spirit of love and cooperation. In Caitlyn's case, what would have been more effective for her and her boss was to say, "Leslie, I know you are having a bad day. What can I do to help you?" That may have shut her down cold. Caitlyn's boss probably wanted someone to argue with her so that she could really take out her frustrations on someone. No one else gave her the opportunity except Caitlyn. Or, Caitlyn could have said, "Excuse me, I'll be with you in a moment. I have to go to the bathroom." Then excuse herself, get herself together, let her boss cool off a little as well, then go back to her boss and say, "Okay, I'm ready to listen. What is it you need me to do for you?"

Then on a calmer day, Caitlyn could revisit the incident and say, "You know, Leslie, I really appreciate the opportunity to work here. I apologize for my behavior the other day. I should not have yelled because we are two adults and we should be able to calmly and rationally discuss any problem like the adults that we are. I will do my part to control my temper and my mouth, okay?" This is how you become the bigger woman. This is how you behave like a virtuous woman. Own up to your part in any negative interaction and vow to God and yourself to do better next time. The apology is more for God and yourself than it is for the other person. Don't concern yourself with issues of the flesh like, "I ain't kissin' nobody's behind!" (which is being prideful) or, "She can kiss my ass!" Not only is this a demonstration of your concern for issues of the flesh, it's straight ghetto, and to become a virtuous woman, you have got to elevate your thinking to be more Christ-like and leave that "me" mentality behind. It's not about you, remember? *It's about what God wants and what God wants for YOU.*

And how about when people get so ill about being passed over for a promotion on the job. They pitch a fit, don't they? And some of them are Christians. You've heard things like, "How dare they promote her over me!" and "They gave her MY job?" What? Really? First of all, let's be real. As long as a person is an employee, she will never own that job. That job belongs to that company and they can do just about whatever they want (within the law) concerning that job, and that employee does not have to approve. Quit thinking "me." Instead, think, "What am I supposed to learn, Lord? What would you have me to do?" Then seek God's will. Remember, it's not about you. *Someone somewhere is watching you, and you have the opportunity to unknowingly bless someone just by the Christ-like behavior you exhibit.*

[VIRTUOUS STEPS]

1. Think of three times your spouse, boyfriend, parents, co-workers, or boss mistreated you by ignoring you, disrespecting you, starting an argument with you, etc. It wasn't really about you, was it? It was about their anger, frustration, or hurt about whatever. In any case, it was THEIR problem, not yours. Did you respond badly? If so, how could you have responded differently that would have helped them? How could you have behaved more Christ-like?
2. Now that you have an alternate way to behave, practice this over and over until it becomes second nature.
3. Remember, you are not to accept or endure abusive behavior. If you are in a physically, mentally, or emotionally abusive situation, get help immediately.

DESIGN YOUR LIFE:
A Lesson in Getting Your Heart's Desires and Living on Purpose

19

"Ask and it will be given to you."~ Matthew 7:7, *Holy Bible*

Sirina is "broke, busted, and disgusted." She has no job, no money, no car, no home, no friends, nothing to do, and nowhere to go. Sirina wonders how she ended up like this. She's been sleeping in her friend's spare bedroom, eating up her friend's food, and borrowing her friend's clothes. Her friend is willing to help her, but this is getting ridiculous! How did she end up like this?

One night, Jessie, Sirina's friend asks, "So, what do you want out of life?" Sirina stared at her blankly and replied, "I don't know." Jessie said, "That's your problem. When you don't know SOMETHING, you can end up with much of NOTHING."

That night before Sirina went to bed, she thought about what Jessie had said. She said her prayers, then went to bed. For the first time in a long time, she had wonderful, abundant dreams. In her dreams she was smiling from ear to ear. She was healthy, happy, and fulfilled. She was confident and at peace. In her dreams, Sirina was blissfully married to a successful Christian man who adored her, she owned a day spa that was so serene it made you feel like you were in heaven. She dreamed of having twins, a boy and a girl, that she buckled safely into her brand new Range Rover so that she could meet up with her sisterfriends for a baby play date. Later, she would return to her modest 4,000 square foot Mediterranean home with her beloved husband and children and settle down for a nice evening in front of the fireplace.

When Sirina awoke the next morning, she was refreshed and ready to start anew. She prayed and meditated on her dream and realized that her dream was what she really wanted (see Daniel 1:17). She began to design her life. She had heard about vision boards and decided she would make one. After cutting up a dozen magazines, and gluing the pictures and words to her poster board, she posted the vision board on the wall in her bedroom. Next, Sirina decided to apply for a job as a receptionist at a day spa in order to earn income and learn the ropes. Then, she decided to apply for financial assistance in order to go to massage therapy school.

Since she had a job now, she began paying her friend for room and board. She shopped at inexpensive stores so that she could afford her own clothes and she started going to church and paying her tithes. Sirina saw that she was blessed.

A few months and a gazillion prayers later, Sirina had successfully completed massage therapy school. She had become a massage therapist at the spa she had been working at and worked closely with the manager so that she would know how to run a spa.

One day she saw a quaint little cottage for sale, purchased it, then converted it into her very own day spa. She called it "Sirina's Sanctuary Day Spa." Her dreams were finally coming true. And guess who walked through the door of her spa? The man who was to be her husband! *She knew what she wanted, so she knew him when she saw him*. Her future husband came through her doors to purchase a gift certificate for his mother for Mother's Day. You know the rest!

You have the power and creativity within you to design the life that you want. In fact, as a child of the Most High God, you are co-creator of your life. Anything you want that's within His will, you can have (see Mark 11:24). Name it and claim it!

Sometimes inspiration can come from a dream, as in Sirina's case. Sometimes it can come from a sermon, a motivational speech, a magazine, a book, sitting in a garden, or from simply searching your heart. Whatever inspires you to act, run with it!

Once you have a dream, a vision for your future, you must act. You must take steps to move yourself toward living the life you have envisioned for yourself. You cannot move without action. Inactivity keeps you in the same place you were in yesterday. It's time to MOVE!

[VIRTUOUS STEPS]

1. Okay. So you have heard of a vision board, right? Like the one that was mentioned in the story above? Get a poster board, glue or tape, scissors, magazines, pictures of yourself, little do-dads, and whatever else you need to make your vision board creative and reflect the life you are designing. Cut out colorful pictures and phrases and glue or tape them to the poster board. This board should come alive! Go to work! When you are done, your vision board should excite and motivate you. Place your vision board in a prominent place so that you can see it several times every day in order to retrain your subconscious mind and inspire you to act. I'm telling you, it works! Let me share this with you: I have had a few vision boards. When I accomplish or obtain many things on my vision board, I create another one. On my last one I had "designed" my husband. I put the date that I would meet him by, the many attributes he would have, what our

relationship would ultimately be like, etc. And guess what? I met him two months after the date on my vision board (I had seen him a lot sooner than that) and we got married 5 ½ months later! I don't recommend that for everyone, but it worked for me! Also, on my newest vision board I claimed that I will be a life coach in the year 2010, and I already have achieved that! I have several other things on my board that I know will come to fruition, too. I'm so excited!

2. Now that your vision board is completed, pray over it. Ask God for what you want and pray for His perfect will to be done. Update your vision board as often as needed.

3. Now write out your goals according to your vision board. Decide what you want your life to be like a year from now. Write out your goals for the year. Then write out your goals for the quarter, then for the month, then for the week, then for the day. As you accomplish a goal, cross it off the list. If you don't accomplish a goal, re-evaluate and re-group and keep it movin'! You will find that the more goals you can check off, the closer you are to living the life you design. You can do it! Now, get it done!

PATIENCE IS A VIRTUE: Lessons in Waiting and Enduring

20

> "With time and patience the mulberry leaf becomes a silk gown."
> ~ Chinese Proverb

Miss Jessie was quite the firecracker when she was younger. She always wanted what she wanted when she wanted it. She knew nothing about waiting for anything. But, through the years, she learned the value of waiting. She learned that good things come to those who wait.

One time, Miss Jessie had inherited a lot of money from a relative who had died. Because she was young, she spent the inheritance on clothes and partying. Ten years later, when Miss Jessie knew better, she realized she could have spent that money on buying a house. At least at that point she would have owned property instead of renting and having those same clothes that had become quite worn through the years.

Then she met her Mr. Right in his early years. They really liked each other, but he wanted to finish his college education before "tying the knot" and she didn't want to wait. They parted ways.

Quite a few years and two deadbeat husbands later, Miss Jessie was a divorcee and no longer partying. Her former Mr. Right had become a successful doctor, and lived a modest life with his one and only wife and their two children. He was reportedly very happy in the suburbs.

Another time Miss Jessie almost went to jail for slapping a woman outside the market. The woman had bumped into her and started talkin' junk. Well, Miss Jessie didn't play that and smacked her right upside her head! The police came and everything. It was a big mess! It certainly wasn't worth risking jail time! Had Miss Jessie exercised a thread of patience, she would have kept calm and composed and would not have entertained the ignorance of the other woman. She would have simply shaken her head at the situation, or ignored it completely, and continued on with her business. She would not have lowered herself to the immaturity of the other woman. She would not have displayed such a lack of class. She would not have seemed like anything other than a Christian.

Miss Jessie has countless other stories of times when it would have been in her best interests to exercise patience (Romans 5:3-4). But, at least in her old age, she has finally learned. She has learned not to react without the benefit of thought. She has learned to hold her tongue when appropriate (Psalm 39:1). She has learned to wait without complaining (Philippians 2:14) and without being anxious. She has learned to wait for the bigger picture and not settle for immediate gratification. She has learned that settling for immediate gratification many times may jeopardize what she may have in the future. *She has learned to endure whatever comes her way, knowing that "this too shall pass."* She has learned to "wait on the Lord and be of good courage (Psalm 27:14)." Miss Jessie has learned.

[VIRTUOUS STEPS]

1. When was the last time you had a conversation with an elderly woman? The next time you get a chance, ask her about what she knows about patience. Ask her to tell you about any lessons she may have learned about having patience. Listen carefully; there is most likely wisdom in her years.
2. Think of a time when you lost your patience. What was it about? How did you feel? What did you do? Think of how you could have handled things differently and the possible consequences of doing things differently.
3. Consider what exercising patience would look like in your life. Consider what YOU would be like if you were a patient woman. Would you be more at peace? Would you have a closer relationship with God? Would you have a deeper understanding of yourself and others? Would you be wiser? Would your life be richer? Would you be able to do more good in the world, or at least in YOUR world? Would you be a better daughter? A better wife? A better mother?
4. Take one day at a time, for the next week, and purposely exercise more patience. Don't speak impulsively. Keep calm, cool, and collected. Don't complain. Have a composed demeanor at all times. Wait for the blessing!

I'VE GOT JOY DOWN IN MY HEART: A Lesson in Joy

21

"Joy is the feeling of grinning on the inside." ~ Dr. Melba Colgrove,
Author

"…And your joy, no one will take from you," John 16:22.
When you look "joy" up in the dictionary, it tells you that joy is
simply "happiness," or something like that. Biblically however, joy
is so much more than happiness or gladness. Joy comes from
communing with God. When you experience this spiritual level of
happiness from your relationship with God, very little else can move
you. You may even glow. People may even say you look "tickled
pink," or that you are letting your "little light shine." Joy is
happiness deep down in your soul. It doesn't depend on your mood,
or anyone else's mood for that matter. It's independent of the daily
grind of your life. It's independent of your career, your bank
account, your trust fund, your college education, your house, your
beautiful children, your Mercedes Benz, or anything else. It's solely
dependent upon your relationship with God.

Do you trust Him? I mean really trust Him? Do you trust
Him with your life? Not just to live, not just to be safe, not just to get

you through, but to order your steps during your days? Do you trust Him to provide for you the desires of your heart at His perfect time? Look at your life. Does your life reflect the trust that you have in God? Or does your life reflect the lack of trust you have in Him? For example, did you pick your mate, or did God do that? Did you pick your job, or did God do that? Did you pick your church, or did God? Did you pick your clothes, or did God? Did you decide what you did last weekend, or did God? Hello, somebody! You cannot experience joy unless you truly, trust God fully, with absolutely all that you are and all that you have.

When you trust God, you're at peace. You don't worry about anything because you know that He's got your back. You know that you will be alright no matter what. The company you work for can announce massive layoffs and you can be at peace because you know that whether you have a job or not, God's got you. You know that if you get laid off, God will provide. You may have to go through some tests to prove that you trust God fully, but you trust that He will never give you more than you can handle (1 Corinthians 10:13). And, you know that if you keep your job, there must be a reason He still has you there, so get busy doing His will. Through your trust in Him, you are at total peace and you have no worries whatsoever.

In order to have joy, you also must believe in God. You must have faith that He can and will do what He says. When He says that "no weapon formed against you shall prosper," (Isaiah 54:17) then you must believe that those that plot against you will not benefit from your woes. When He says He will provide you with your own transportation and your own food, (Isaiah 58:14), you must have faith that it will come to pass. We must have faith when God tells us that He is giving us land (Exodus 6:8). We must believe that He "gives us richly all things to enjoy." (1 Timothy 6:17) We must have faith in God! Only our Creator is "tried and true." He is the only perfect being, flawless, and incapable of lying. If we believe anyone, we must believe Him. We cannot experience joy without having unshakable faith in our Lord. Walk in this faith, live in this faith, and you will be on the path to unspeakable joy.

When you have joy, you are living for God; your life is in divine order, you are on purpose, and you are at complete peace, trusting in God, having faith in His Word, and experiencing the joy that only He can bring (Psalms 4: 7-8), joy that no one can take from you.

[VIRTUOUS STEPS]

1. Reaching the spiritual level of joy in the Lord requires that you become dead to the flesh; i.e. embrace your spiritual being and deny your humanly (flesh) being. Think of one way you can move towards experiencing joy today. How can you deepen your trust, peace, and faith in God? What do you have today that you can surrender to Him in order to develop that deep relationship with Him that can lead to your joy, even in your sorrow?
2. I challenge you to give up just one way that you KNOW, that you KNOW, that you KNOW you are living in sin. Give it over to God, leave it at the altar. Commit to Him and trust and believe that He will lead you down a better path, a path that will lead to ultimate peace and joy.
3. Build up your "faith muscles." How? By listening to the word of God (Romans 10:17) over and over and over again. The more you listen, the more you believe, and that goes for anything! So, a word to the wise: be careful what you listen to, because eventually you will believe it on some level. Choose to listen (and read) the Word of God so that you will grow to have faith in what He says

to you. When you believe, you will begin to trust, then you can experience the peace and joy that follows.

SURROUND YOURSELF WITH POSITIVE, PROGRESSIVE PEOPLE:
A Lesson in Choosing Your Company Wisely

22

"Tell me what company you keep and I'll tell you what you are."
~ Miguel de Cervantes Saavedra, Spanish Novelist and Poet

Who are your runnin' partners? Who are your aces? Now, consider what these friends have going on. Are they like you? Are they making moves to go places? Are they making progress with their goals? Are they driving you forward? Or, are they exactly where they were five years ago? Have they been complaining about the same job, same boyfriend, same house, same car, same family drama for the last five years? Are they sucking you, your energy, your time, or your bank account dry?

News flash: The people you hang with, the people you spend time around or listening to, will do one of two things. *They will either help lift you up or ultimately bring you down.* These people may be friends from grade school, church people, co-workers, or family. It doesn't matter. Whoever you are around for considerable amounts of time will knowingly or unknowingly influence your life, and at times, the decisions you make in your life.

So, think about it. Who do college students primarily hang with? Other college students, right? And who do corporate Americans primarily hang with? Other professionals, right? People tend to socialize with people who are either in the same place in their lives as they are, or people who are where they intend to go. For instance, a physical therapy student may socialize primarily with other P.T. students, physical therapists, or other healthcare workers. Actresses primarily have other actors and actresses in their circle. Christians have fellowship with other Christians. Who is in your circle of influence?

Why is this so? Because people who have a plan for their lives and recognize their value realize that socializing with likeminded people will only enhance their growth and help them to enhance the growth of those with whom they are socializing (see Philippians 2:2). Does this mean that a pilot and a lawyer cannot be good friends and hang out? No. Both are professionals and both have careers, even though the careers are different. They are both career-oriented. Will a teacher hang out with a homeless woman? Probably not (unless the teacher was mentoring the homeless woman, and that's a different chapter). While the teacher may be able to contribute to the homeless woman's well-being, the homeless woman is probably in no position to add to the teacher's life. The relationship is typically not considered to be mutually beneficial.

Take these three friends, for instance. Mischa grew up with Linda and Sonja. Mischa went to college to become a veterinarian, Linda went to college to become an accountant, and Sonja got pregnant so she dropped out, had baby daddy drama, and ended up on welfare to support her child. One year after high school, the girls got together to reminisce about old times. They had a great conversation until they talked about the present. Mischa and Linda talked about how hard finals were, how cute college boys were, how wild some of the parties could be, pledging, how much home has changed, etc. Sonja just listened. When the other two came up for air, Sonja talked about how expensive diapers were, her baby daddy drama, his new girlfriend, how she was down to her last $20 which had to last her a week. While Sonja's monologue was fairly interesting, Mischa and Linda just could not identify, they couldn't relate. They wanted to help Sonja, so they asked her what she wanted to do with her life. Strangely enough, Sonja was somewhat satisfied with her life although she complained. She didn't want to do anything different with her life. They tried to support her emotionally, but they had no basis for supplying this kind of support as they had not experienced anything remotely close to her life, nor did they want to.

After their get-together was over, they vowed to stay in touch. For a while, all three tried, but eventually it ended up that Mischa and Linda kept in closer touch. They visited each other at school, talked on the phone about class, potential boyfriends, and trips they wanted to take. Sonja ended up wanting to borrow money, have Mischa and Linda miss exams to babysit, have them help her spy on baby daddy, couldn't go on any trips unless they paid for it, and still didn't want to do anything else. Mischa and Linda eventually stopped keeping in touch with Sonja except for the occasional call to "just check on her."

Another year went by. Mischa and Linda had finished their sophomore year and were still good friends. Sonja was pregnant again and in jail. She and some of her other friends were serving time for viciously beating up her baby daddy's girlfriend and vandalizing her car and house.

If Mischa and Linda had been with Sonja when she committed these crimes, they may have been arrested as well. And not only that, they may have lost their scholarships and been expelled from school. Mischa and Linda knew they could not help Sonja because she didn't want their kind of help. So, they had to let her go. They continued to support each other and continued to progress with their lives. They understood that they could not "bring Sonja up" and that Sonja could instead "bring them down."

[VIRTUOUS STEPS]

1. Have you made the decision to progress in your life? Do you have goals? Is anyone speaking negatively to you? Is anyone holding you back? Who are the naysayers? It's time to do some housekeeping and cut some folks back in your life. Maybe not cut them OUT if you can't. But cut those negative, go-nowhere people back! Maybe you haven't progressed any further in your life than you have because of the negative energy, negative messages, or bad advice you have been getting from negative, slack, trifling, or lazy people. Stop listening! Stop spending all that time with them! Why would you listen to a woman tell you about how to treat your husband when she's been married and divorced four times? Why would you listen to a woman tell you how to discipline your son when she's got six boys and all of them are in jail? Think! Make a list of everyone you need to cut back or cut out of your life. End those toxic relationships. If they aren't positive and progressive, you don't need them and they don't need you! *Remember, you can't help someone that doesn't want to be helped!* Let them go and move on to folks who are either where you are or where you want to be!

2. Make a list of people you admire. List why you admire them. If they are people that you know personally, then seek to spend more time around them. If you do not know them personally, then read all about them, listen to their speeches, and spend time with their material. Let their

greatness shape you, but remember, nobody's perfect.

KEEP GOD FIRST IN YOUR LIFE:
A Lesson in Keeping Your Head On Straight

23

"But, seek ye first the kingdom of God and His righteousness and all these things will be added unto you." ~ Matthew 6:33, *Holy Bible*

People, being human, tend to focus on "the desires of their heart" and have less focus on the Lord. We tend to focus on what we don't have, rather than on what we do have. At times, we can even be consumed with what we want, to the point where most of our energy is directed towards those desires.

I've noticed this preoccupation more frequently when it comes to relationships. We women tend to focus on the man and the relationship more than we focus on God. If we don't have a Boaz, we wonder where he is, what he's like, what our life will be like when he arrives, how he looks, feels, smells, etcetera, etcetera. Or, if we have a man, we become very concerned with pleasing him. Heaven forbid he's acting up. Then we are preoccupied with why he's acting up, how he could treat us so badly, what's wrong with him, why he doesn't love us the way we love him, where the affection and devotion are, why won't he help out around the house, yada yada yada.

God absolutely will give us the desires of our hearts when we are obedient to Him and have a clean heart. But, one thing the Bible commands us to do BEFORE we are to have what we want is to seek God. Go after God (Luke 10:27) and all of His righteousness and THEN He will add all of those other things (even a Boaz) unto us.

Janelle is like many women. She's a good Christian woman who's unhappily married. She spends day in and day out, weeks at a time, serving her man and he is very unappreciative of her devotion. Janelle believes that she's not receiving the love from her husband because she's either not doing the right thing or not doing enough of the right thing, so she literally wears herself out trying to gain favor with her husband. She works outside their home, takes care of their three children, helps pay the bills, cooks nightly, cleans every other day, and has sex as often as he wants without complaint. Even still, with all of that, she cries every day because her heart is unfulfilled because of the lack of a loving response from her husband. He doesn't give her the random forehead kisses; he doesn't give her hugs "just because," he doesn't compliment her on her beauty or even seem to notice how she looks. He doesn't ever hold her hand, rub her feet, or send a smile her way. He doesn't even have pleasant conversations with her. Romance? No, that never crosses his mind. The more Janelle does, the worse she feels. What's wrong with this picture?

Janelle knows the Lord, but she doesn't spend a whole lot of time with Him. Why? Because she's too busy trying to please her husband! She's so busy trying to win his attention and affection that she is neglecting the most important relationship she has and ever will have, and she's suffering for it. God needs to be first in her life. Janelle needs to reconnect with God and His purpose for her life. She needs to go about doing God's work and let God handle her marriage. She needs to continue to live virtuously, and what Janelle does not accomplish with her marriage, she must leave for God to do, because only He can.

When you have other things or people before God, including your marriage, that's the equivalent of "serving other gods" and "putting other gods before Me." And when you serve other gods, you become enslaved to them. The Bible teaches us that you cannot "serve two masters" (Matthew 6:24) because you will love one and despise the other. This is essentially what Janelle has done by putting her marriage before God instead of putting her marriage in His hands.

Backing off and letting God handle her marriage is a test of her faith. How can she back off and leave her marriage in God's hands? She must actively seek God's purpose for her life and begin to live on purpose. She must pray fervently for guidance in where to go and what to do, and clarity so that she will understand what it is that she must do, not do, or learn. Should she continue to pray for her marriage? Absolutely! But worrying (worrying is not of God) about her marriage should not consume her.

Another thing, God is supposed to be part of the marriage anyway! "A three-strand cord is not easily broken (Ecclesiastes 4:12)." She must not only pray for her marriage, but invite God into her home and into her marriage. If possible, she and her husband must pray, worship, and study the Bible together. That is the only way to build and strengthen the three-strand cord. Otherwise, there is nothing that she can do alone that will give her the kind of marriage that she longs for.

Here's another tip: *Don't ever lose yourself in a man* (more on this in the upcoming chapter). If you get lost, lose yourself in God. Always stay connected to God and the woman He has called you to be with the purpose He has set before you. Continue to live your life. Just because Janelle is also Mrs. Smith does not mean she ceases to be Janelle. God created Janelle who has her own individual interests and her own God-given purpose. Janelle can still be herself and be a wife to her husband. It's called balancing your life and making it work. When God is included in the marriage, the husband and wife will complement each other and fit together like a glove, even with their separate interests and purposes. God can make it happen like that. Isn't He awesome?

[VIRTUOUS STEPS]

Finish these sentences:

1. I am worrying about my marriage because….

2. I cannot change my husband, but I can change my approach to our marriage by….

3. I can include God in my marriage by….

4. I can back off and let God handle it by….

5. My God-given purpose in life is....

6. I can continue to walk in my purpose by….

7. The fruits of the Spirit that I need to embody and embrace in order to get through this trying time are….

DATE YOURSELF: A Lesson in Self-Love and Pampering

24

"I don't like myself, I'm crazy about myself!"~ Mae West, Actress

Ladies, how many times have we wanted a man to give us flowers, rub our tired feet, or cook us a special meal? And, exactly how many times have we done that for ourselves? Uh huh. That's what I thought.

We need to spend time loving and caring for ourselves the way we want our men to love us. Take Portia, for instance. Portia loves to spend time with herself. She plans one whole day per month to just do Portia. On "Portia Day," she goes to her favorite day spa and gets a hot oil scalp treatment with scalp massage, a seaweed body wrap, a deluxe pedicure, a gel nail fill-in, a 60-minute exfoliating facial, and a 90-minute hot stone massage. While at the day spa, she is treated with a very healthy lunch with a mineral water. She feels like she is in heaven. Portia understands the importance of taking care of herself and treating herself to some uninterrupted pampering time. She knows that pampering is good for the soul and is therefore a necessity in order for her to maintain a happy, balanced lifestyle.

After she leaves the spa, she enjoys a walk by the lake, then ends her day at the florist where she buys herself a single, long stem red rose. Now that's self-love!

Felecia also enjoys self-pampering, on a budget. And trust me, there's absolutely everything right with pampering on a budget! Felecia blocks off four hours early on Saturday in order to treat herself. She puts a clay mask on her face, exfoliates her hands and files her nails. Then she paints a clear coat of polish on her newly trimmed nails. Because she likes her feet to be cute, she soaks her feet in sea salt, scrubs away dead skin with a pumice stone, clips and files her toenails, massages cream into her feet to ward off excessive dryness, then polishes her toenails a flattering color. Felecia also enjoys plucking her eyebrows. She's discovered that as long as her eyebrows are defined, she can get away with wearing a natural shade of lip color as her only makeup.

After she has had her pampering time, she drives to her favorite chocolate store with the sunroof open and buys herself a delectable box of chocolates. Fabulous!

Monica, on-the-other-hand, does little things to treat herself every day. She showers with "the good shower gel," rubs her feet down every night with special foot cream, eats dinner on the "good dishes" by candlelight with the television off and only jazz playing in the background. When she's feeling down, she buys herself a greeting card and mails it to herself. A day or two later when it arrives, she smiles, happy that it is something other than a bill. And right on time! Other days she dances by herself to her favorite 70's music. She turns the music on blast and dances around the living room like a crazy woman! Now that's fun!

Monica also buys herself balloons and flowers, goes to the park, zoo, movies, out to eat, and to the circus by herself----she always makes sure she's safe and doesn't go out too late. Sometimes she hangs out with her girlfriends and cherishes her time with her guy friends, but she doesn't have anyone special in her life. And at this great time in her life, that's just fine with her!

Then there's Danielle. Danielle is in self-neglect mode. Day in and day out, week in and week out, months go by and she STILL does not spend any quality time caring for herself. She can't tell you what a foot rub feels like. She doesn't know if she likes walks in the park or by the lake. She doesn't know if she would prefer candy or flowers. She's never had anyone send her a nice card in the mail and she's never eaten on anyone's good dishes. She's never enjoyed a sunrise or a sunset. She hasn't been treating herself to "living" on any level. She spends each day simply existing and surviving. If she doesn't find the time to care for herself in these ways, why should anyone else find the time to care for her? She has got to learn to enjoy being with herself and pampering herself before she can give her gift of companionship and love to anyone else and expect it in return.

Ladies, you have got to get "full," as the old folks say, so that you can give some to someone else. You cannot give from a place of emptiness. Have you ever tried it? And how has that worked for you?

In order to be the woman that God created you to be, you must first learn to love God, then yourself. Then you can "love your neighbor as you love yourself." How can you say, "I love the Lord," but then don't demonstrate self-love? Be courageous enough to regularly celebrate yourself. You are worth it!

[VIRTUOUS STEPS]

1. Food for thought: When was the last time you pampered yourself, treated yourself, or showed yourself any measure of love? What did you do? How did you feel?

2. Decide three ways you want to show yourself love and pamper yourself within the next seven days. It can be as simple as using an upscale body care product during your bedtime ritual and savoring the experience, scheduling a Brazilian wax (if that's your thang), or treating yourself to a frozen yogurt. The sky is the limit!

3. Remember how we used to write cute little love notes as kids? Get a colorful sticky notepad and write a few little love notes to yourself. Write wonderfully positive things to yourself such as "you are beautiful" or "I love you" or "hang in there!" Post them on your bathroom mirror, on the refrigerator, on your door, on your television, in your car...wherever!

4. Make a list of nice things you would like to do for others this year. Do some of these things for yourself while you are doing them for others. Make a game of it. How many things can you think of? How many people can you bless in addition to yourself? For example, you can buy a perfume for yourself and one for your mom. Or, you can go wall climbing and treat your best friend, too. Notice how you feel. You should start to feel special, and should feel good knowing that you are helping others to feel loved and appreciated as well.

LET'S TALK ABOUT SEX, BABY!:
A Lesson in the Perils of Premarital Sex

25

"Let's talk about all the good things and the bad things that may be."
~ Salt & Pepa

Nowadays, it seems that almost every unmarried adult is having sex. According to the Bible, sex before marriage is fornication and fornication is forbidden. The Bible tells us to "Flee fornication. Every sin that a man doeth is without the body; but he that committeth fornication sinneth against his own body (1 Corinthians 6:18)."

Sidebar: I'm not "holier than thou." I fully understand how it is out in the world as I was a willing participant in fornication. I had my share and probably yours too, however, I knew it was wrong, but was not usually compelled to stop. I didn't fully understand how this sin against myself and God could so adversely affect my life. I fully understand now, and will try to explain it to you.

Let's start at the very beginning. Let's examine what you first thought about sex. Was it something you saw in a movie that was romanticized and caused you to think that that was what love was? Did some cute little boy tell you that he loved you so you let him woo your panties off? Were you lonely, oftentimes alone, left to read adult books which taught you that sex was what happened when people loved each other? (Remember Harlequin Romance novels?) Was your father absent from your life so you learned about love and sex in all the wrong places? Did you learn from your mom, aunt, or cousin that sex is what you gave to get what you want?

Many times, for women, sex has emotional origins. We first decided to have sex not because of what we consciously thought about sex, but because of how we felt about it. We made the decision to have sex based on how we felt about what we thought. We may have equated sex with love, attention, or affection—things that we need as girls and continue to need as grown women. These feelings, these desires, if not satisfied in a healthy way, a godly way, give way to the devil.

After eating the apple from the forbidden tree, it's hard to put it back down, it becomes addictive. So we continue, believing that we are satisfied and getting the love, attention, or affection that we want, when in fact, we are not. You see, when you have sex, soul ties can form. A soul tie is a where a bond is formed between souls. So, whenever you have sex with someone, you are giving them a piece of your soul. 1 Corinthians 6:16 says, "What? Know ye not that he which is joined to an harlot is one body? For two, saith he, shall be one flesh." Not only do you leave a piece of yourself with them, they leave a piece of themselves with you. Many times what's transferred between souls, especially outside of marriage, is not anything good. For example, if you're relatively sane and you have sex with a crazy man, you may later experience his craziness. Think of it like this: he literally plugs into you to both make a deposit and a withdrawal— and you let him, or them, whichever the case may be. You put yourself at risk for not only sexually transmitted diseases and pregnancies, but also make yourself available and susceptible to any mental and emotional baggage he has…as if you haven't had enough of your own.

Soul ties are oftentimes the reasons we find it hard to let go of someone who we know is not good for us. We take mental, emotional, sexual, and physical abuse from terrible men because of the soul ties we allowed to form from having sex with them. It's just not worth the few seconds of orgasm we experienced (if we had one), now is it? And some people think that God is being too strict when it comes to premarital or extramarital sex saying that "it's natural and okay as long as these grown people love each other or want each other," etc. So, it's okay to spread yourself a little here and a little there? So it's okay to give up your body and possibly your sanity for some short-lived "love?" In this day and age where the divorce rate in America is 50%, how is it that we actually believe that this man who we are not married to will actually love us forever and is worthy of our all when the divorced women are positive proof that this "love" doesn't last forever? So, you love each other, but just not enough to get married? What, you think marriage will "ruin" your relationship? It's all a trick of the enemy on every level, and we all fall right into it.

As a virtuous woman, you absolutely must make a conscious decision to repent for this sin, break all soul ties that have formed between you and them, and pray for complete healing and restoration. We ask God for what we want, but we oftentimes are not willing to live within His will. We ask God for a husband that will be faithful and true to us, however, we are not faithful and true to God and ourselves when it comes to sex, so how dare we ask for anything? We must also live like we are ready for what we want instead of simply asking for it. Let me put it like this: If your child asked you for a car that you could afford, but had not proven that she could drive it or would even be responsible for it, would you give it to her? Ummm, that's a "no." So why do we expect God to give us our husband when we freely give ourselves to other men? And even when we get our husbands, we expect and hope for the "happily ever after" when we have pieces of ourselves scattered across America (he does, too) and have our souls tied to Tom, Dick, and Harry. It's crazy! No wonder the divorce rate is so high! We need to, at some point, stop the madness and take a stand for God, the Bible, ourselves, and our future marriages so that our families can flourish and weather the storms. We need to bring God into our relationships thereby bringing the divorce rate down. It starts with you. It starts with me.

Yes, you're a grown woman. Yes, you have the human right and choice to fornicate if you want. But, as a saved Christian woman who accepted Jesus Christ as her Lord and Savior, after He died for YOU, do you really have the *right* to willingly commit this sin against yourself and Him? Yes, you have the choice, but do you really have that *right*? Hmmm…that's something for you to think about.

If you accept your body as the temple and the Lord lives inside of you, can't you see that the only time you should have sex is when it's with your husband, within the confines of a union that He has blessed? That way, you only have God and your husband to be a part of you.

Unless Jesus comes back right now, it's not too late to make a change. Before I got married, I made the decision to abstain from sex until I got married. Well, I met my husband and incorrectly rationalized (we tend to wrongly do that when it's something we want) that "I know I'm going to marry him anyway, so I may as well." And we did get married—quickly. The Bible says, "But if they cannot contain, let them marry: for it is better to marry than to burn" (1 Corinthians 7:9). So, I did the right thing by getting married, but I later paid the cost for the sin of fornicating with him (remember, you will reap what you sow). You see, I knew better and did it anyway. Remember we just discussed soul ties and transference of baggage? Uh huh…enough said. (Don't get me wrong, my husband is a great guy. I truly believe he is heaven sent. I also truly believe that I had a part in making things a lot harder than they had to be. I urge you not to make the same mistake.)

[VIRTUOUS STEPS]

1. What long term benefits do you think you get from having premarital sex? If you listed any long term benefits, are they holy? For that matter, what holy short term benefits do you get?
2. Write down your thoughts about the following question. Since God created marriage and sex and designed it to be holy, is it any wonder that neither marriage nor sex truly works without Him?
3. Many times we have sex because we are tempted by people, places, and things. What are some of the places and things that cause you to be tempted? Who are the people that tempt you? In what ways can you avoid temptation?
4. As a single woman, if you were to achieve this level of virtue, what would this mean in your life?
5. If you are a single or married woman who had premarital or extramarital sex, consider having a soul washing or spend some time reading reputable Christian books and websites about soul ties and how to break them.
6. What would have to happen in order for you to give up fornication? HIV/AIDS, hepatitis, gonorrhea, chlamydia, herpes, vaginal warts, mental and physical abuse, and heartbreak are already prevalent in America. What's it going to take for YOU to stop fornicating?

7. Study 1 Corinthians 6:9-11, 15-20; 1 Corinthians 7:2; and 1 Corinthians 10:13.

NO SHACKING, PERIOD!:
A Lesson in Living in Your Own Space

26

"God's great cosmic joke on the human race was requiring that men and women live together in marriage."
~ Mark Twain, American Author

When do you go to a shoe store, find the perfect shoes, and they allow you to walk out of the store with the explanation that you will pay for them later, IF they work out for you? Or, when are you able to go to a homebuilder to have a house built and they build it and let you move in without you signing a contract? It just doesn't happen. You are required to purchase the shoes before leaving the store, if you want the shoes. Likewise, you are required to sign a contract on the house, if you want to move into your home. A certain level of commitment is expected and required in order to make these transactions.

So, why is it that some women allow themselves to settle for less than a commitment, i.e., marriage, from their man before they live with him? When a woman lives with a man before marriage, she is allowing him to "walk out of the store without buying the shoes" and "move into the house without signing a contract." Isn't she worth more than that?

Ask yourself this: what would a woman typically do for her man if she lived with him before marrying him? Now, consider what would typically do for her husband after they got married? What's the difference? If there is no difference, then why on earth would he want to marry her if he gets everything from her without getting married? And where exactly is the commitment (from him) in that? If a woman gives a man the very best of her, he must show her that he deserves her by "puttin' a ring on it," that is, by marrying her. If he does not commit to spending the rest of his life with her via holy matrimony, then he is not worth shackin' with, period.

Cameron is an intelligent woman that most people consider "decent" looking. She's single with no children, a great cook, holds a high paying corporate position at a Fortune 500 company, wears designer clothing, has a quirky sense of humor, is a "people" person, keeps a clean house, loves to travel, is fun-loving, affectionate, and reliable. Cameron has also "shacked" with three different men and married none. Somewhere around the year and a half mark things turn sour in her relationships. Up until they break up, each of the men say they are in love with her; that they want to marry her "one day" but that day never comes. She cooked for them, cleaned for them, paid bills with them, had sex with them, and supported them in their endeavors. She played "wifey." No wonder she was devastated when they broke up! She had given her all to each of them and was left with nothing but cheap feelings and wasted time when they split. *She was a wife to no husband.* Her self-esteem suffered. She started thinking thoughts like, "Why wouldn't any of them marry me? What's wrong with me? Why can't I find anyone? Nobody's going to ever love me. I give my all and it's still not good enough."

To make matters worse, all three of these guys left stating that they were in love with someone else—someone who, by the way, they did NOT live with before marrying them. How's that for a good slap in the face?

See, when a woman lives with a man before marrying him, she plays wife to him and gives him the best of her without getting a husband in return. This arrangement is out of the will of God. The *Holy Bible* says, "Wives, submit yourselves unto your own husbands as unto the Lord (Ephesians 5:22)." When a woman shacks, she is being a wife and submitting herself to a man who is not her husband. The Bible commands, "Husbands, love your wives.... (Ephesians 5:25)." Since this man knows he is not her husband, he does not recognize her as his wife, (although he is more than willing to let her play the role of his wife) and therefore, does not have to love her as such. Face it: if he loved her as his wife, he would make her his wife, period.

Cameron met another seemingly wonderful man. They dated for a while, then as in her previous cohabiting relationships, this new wonderful man asked her if they could live together to "try it out." Cameron finally learned her lesson. She wasn't about to "give the milk away for free" and he obviously wasn't ready to "buy the cow." She told him no. She explained to Mr. Wonderful that she was interested in dating and getting married and nothing in-between. She made it clear that the only man she would be living with was her husband. Mr. Wonderful was perplexed, but said he understood. He really liked her, so they continued dating while remaining in separate homes. Two short years later, Cameron and Mr. Wonderful got married!

Shacking can leave a woman with low(er) self-esteem, feeling trapped, unwanted, unloved, unworthy, angry, hurt, and used. If she is a Christian, she may feel that her life is off balance and she may even feel convicted since she knows she is out of the will of God. Clearly, there is nothing about shacking that is virtuous. Shacking is out of the will of God, so praying that God will "bless that union" is a waste of time because God does not bless or condone sin of any nature for any reason, ever. So what can the shacking woman do? Work to come into alignment with the will of God so that He can bless her with the husband He has for her. It may be the man she is shacking with, or it may not be. Only He knows. But the longer she is out of the will of God, the longer she delays her blessings.

[VIRTUOUS STEPS]

1. If you are a single woman who is shacking with her man, do one of two things: marry him or one of you move out. Don't forget to repent for this sin, and vow not to fall into this trap of the enemy again. In fact, watch for it because Satan will most likely tempt you with this particular sin again. Why wouldn't he? It worked before!

2. Take time to consider what a woman gains when she remains a girlfriend living separate from her man instead of playing wife to a man that isn't her husband. She maintains her sense of independence and self-reliance, her self-respect, self-esteem, dignity, integrity, sense of self-worth, and most importantly, she remains in God's will in this matter. Can you think of any other personal benefits to living in your own space until marriage?

3. List some of the temptations you may have to shack with someone. Once you have listed these temptations, identify the root of the temptation, then snatch each temptation up by the root. For example, you may be tempted to live with your man because the two of you can split the bills. The root of this temptation may be that you are afraid that you won't be able to afford paying your bills on your own just because you had a hard time paying bills in the past. Snatch that root out! Call it out! Then pray on a solution. Pray that you find a way to

make more money, and/or that you can cut your expenses, for example. Learn to trust God who will provide for you according to His riches and glory.

MY "MR. RIGHT" IS A BOAZ:
A Lesson in Setting Standards for Mate Selection

27

"…He has not stopped showing his kindness to the living and the
dead…."
~ Ruth 2:20, *Holy Bible*

One thing that we tend to do is set our standards high, but as
soon as a fine man smiles our way, we relax those standards. Our
loneliness, desire for a mate, desire for sex, desire for children, or
our need for someone to help us with the bills drives us to "settle"
for just a "fine man." I sincerely hope if you are at this point in the
book, that you have come to the full realization of your value and
have stopped selling yourself short by wasting time on the first
warm, nice-looking body that comes along.

So, assuming that you are now a woman of virtue, you must
settle for no less than your Boaz. Boaz is your standard for your
mate, that is, for your boyfriend /fiancé/husband. What are the
character traits of your God-fearing Boaz? Your Boaz is self-
sufficient. He has his OWN: his own home, his own transportation,
his own food, his own clothes, his own legitimate source of income,
and he pays his own bills.

Your Boaz has a good reputation. Good people speak well of him and he's not wanted by the police or government for anything. He's strong-willed (but submits to God and his woman, just as she submits to him), and commands respect of which he gets and gives. He's not lazy; he works hard at working smart. He accepts responsibility for himself (including his actions) and his family, which means he spends time with his children (if he has any) and supports them financially. He clearly demonstrates that he values himself and his family. He's confident, but his confidence lies in God and not himself.

Now, when it comes to you, his virtuous woman, he will pursue you. You may have to very subtly get his attention so that he knows you exist (simply cross his path), but once he knows you're alive, if he is the man for you, he will pursue you. Remember, "Whoso findeth a wife findeth a good thing (Proverbs 8:22)…?" Obviously your man is meant to find you, to pursue you.

As he is pursuing you, pay attention to his character…do your homework. What kind of reputation does he have? Where does he work? How long has he been in his field, at that particular job, and does he also own his own business? Who are his friends? What are they like? Keep in mind the old saying, "Birds of a feather flock together." If he hangs with bums, he may be a bum in disguise.

How does he treat women? For that matter, how does he treat his mama and other women in his family? How long has it been since he's been in a committed relationship? (If he just ended a two-year relationship two months ago, he may not be ready for you, so take your time developing your friendship. Give him time to fully get over his last woman and their relationship, so that he can make a fresh start with you, if that's the natural progression of your friendship.)

Okay. So he's pursuing you and you're keeping your eyes wide open just as a virtuous woman does. If he is a Boaz, he will recognize that you are a virtuous woman (because he is selective) and he will work to win your affection and your approval of him as your mate. He will prove himself to be an honest man, trustworthy, loyal, faithful, and kind-hearted. He's supportive of you and cares about the things and people that you care about.

He's honorable; he does the right thing. He's generous and caring. He speaks well of you and to you. He protects you, provides for you, comforts you, blesses you, and appreciates you. He loves you.

It sounds like he's perfect, right? It may sound that way, but remember: there are no perfect men, but there may be one who is perfect for you.

The man who approaches you who seems to be your Boaz, may end up being just a good friend. Here's an important point to remember: When you meet a man, start with *friend* in mind, not husband. When you start with *friend* in mind, you're starting from the beginning and taking the time to get to know him. That's starting at point A and working towards point B. You take time to observe him and go through a sort of mental checklist to see if he is possibly your Boaz. If you find out something unsavory about him, such as the fact that he has 20 kids and is paying child support for none, then you can halt things and keep him at friend, maybe.

When you start with *husband* in mind, you are starting at point D and working back towards point A and trying to force him into fitting into the box. You're not taking time to observe him or his life before you think of him as your husband, so when you find out about his 20 kids and his paying child support for none, you are either hurt that you must now let him go, or worse yet, you decide to become his savior and help him "do the right thing" and pay child support for his 20 kids because you love him and are destined to be with him. Seriously? And we wonder why we end up feeling used and abused! We allow ourselves to walk into messes like this! Set your standards (the Bible is great for helping you with this) and stick to them. Let your new man show you if he's your Boaz while you all along continue to be the virtuous woman that your Boaz is looking for.

[VIRTUOUS STEPS]

1. Examine your reasons for wanting a man, or better yet, a Boaz. See if your reasons are pure or if they are selfish. Finish this sentence: "I want a Boaz because…"
2. Consider not only what partnering with such a man would be like, but consider also how you can enhance his life. Remember, it's not all about you. Finish this sentence: "I can enhance my man's life by…"
3. Become familiar with Ruth (a virtuous woman) and Boaz as they are written about in the *Holy Bible*. Read the story of Ruth and Boaz in Ruth, chapters 1-4. Embrace this story. Pay attention to how virtuous she was, how she lived her life, and also note how Boaz lived his life, took care of people and things, and handled business honorably. Notice how they did things *in order*.
4. Do you know of any Boazes? List them. What makes them a Boaz? Just as there are women who everyday strive to be virtuous, there are also men who everyday strive to be like Boaz.
5. Finish this sentence: "The areas I need to grow in in order to be ready for my Boaz are…"

DON'T LOSE YOURSELF IN YOUR MAN: A Lesson in Preserving Your SELF

28

"Don't compromise yourself. You are all you've got." ~ Janis Joplin, American Singer

Have you ever lost yourself in a man? Did your whole entire life revolve around him? Did you eat, drink, sleep, and breathe him? Were all of your waking hours consumed by him? Did you lose interest in activities that used to please you? Did you stop hanging out with your girlfriends because you wanted to be up under him? If you answered "yes" to even one of these questions, you may have lost yourself in that man.

Yes, that's pretty bad, but hey, most of us have been down that road before. We are so in love; we just have to be so close to him, like we are actually joined to him. Shoot, we want to breathe the same air that he breathes! Yes, we've had it bad! But, if we've been down that road before, hopefully, we learned something that first time around. However, if we didn't, we are destined to make the same mistakes again, so let's nip it now.

Your man, if he was a good one, was attracted to the goodness he saw in you. He admired your intelligence and the fact that you had your own opinion. He appreciated your independence and the fact that you weren't needy or clingy. He was happy that you had your own life with your own friends, which meant you had something else to do besides worry about his every move. He was in awe of your talents, and loved to watch you do your thang. You were strong, confident, and commanded respect. You were your own woman, and he was thankful for that.

This "goodness" that attracted him, this goodness that is inside of you is what you must hang onto, what you must continue to focus on so that you can grow every day. You must continue to let the world see yourSELF every day. This is the woman God created, not to hide under a man's armpit, but to shine brightly so that the world can see and know of His goodness---through you.

So, if you feel yourself becoming obsessed with your man, *step away from the man now*! Take a "me time out" and get ahold of yourself, woman! Regroup, refocus, and reconnect with yourSELF. Do things you enjoy doing. Work on fulfilling your God-given purpose. Reconnect with people you say you love, but haven't seen or spoken with in a while. Take some time to "do YOU."

Let's take a look at Zoe. She's bright, energetic, has a great sense of humor, regularly volunteers at the soup kitchen, has a great sense of humor, and loves animals. Zoe radiates love everywhere she goes; people love being around her. Her lifelong dream was to become a social worker and work with teenage girls. And then she met her Adonis.

This man was everything Zoe ever thought she wanted, and more. He was extremely tall, remarkably good-looking, and genuinely into the Word of God. This man was intelligent, ambitious, successful, independent, and embodied all the fruit of the spirit, not to mention cultured—he spoke five different languages. A nice catch he was.

He appreciated the beauty in Zoe, not just that her smile was electric or that she laughed at his silly jokes, he appreciated her sense of humanity. He marveled at how much she wanted to help people and how helping people gave her great joy. But then, he noticed that she was too willing to give up her volunteer Saturdays to be with him. She wanted to go part-time in school instead of full-time, and she started wondering what he was doing that was so important that he couldn't be with her since she was sacrificing her life to be with him. To her dismay, their whirlwind romance was coming to a screeching halt. She couldn't figure out why.

Here's why: Zoe was losing herself in her man. She used to like volunteering at the soup kitchen. Now she'd rather stay at home watching a game on TV with him (which, by the way, he enjoyed doing with the fellas). Before, she had goals, dreams, and aspirations for her life apart from his, but now she seemed to be content with meshing with his life. He once saw her as a strong mate, a potential wife. He thought that if he "joined forces" with her, they could be a power couple and "take on the world." Now, she just seemed like "every other woman" to him.

Zoe needs to stay on task. Her life was going in a particular direction before him, and it is still supposed to go in that same direction, not disappear! It's okay to be enamored with a godly man; however, a virtuous woman must always be herself and live HER life. A virtuous woman stays true to herself and does not lay down her God-given purpose for any man. If the man is for her, he will complement her and she will complement him. They can both be individuals TOGETHER.

[VIRTUOUS STEPS]

1. Take inventory of your own dreams, goals, and aspirations. Write them down. Go to work on them.

2. Take time to discover your purpose if you don't already know what it is.
3. Step away from the man! Take some time apart doing things that you have always wanted to do. Work on a project. Write a book. Go on a spiritual retreat with some girlfriends. Go to Bible Study. Join the Usher Board at church. Whatever you do, get out of his armpit!

EPILOGUE

Writing this book has been such an eye-opener for me. I am not perfect. Much of what I have written is based on what I have learned and am still learning as I strive to practice virtuous living every day. I am just like you; I still make mistakes. When extremely frustrated, I may curse…I am still working on this and am getting better. Although rare, there are still times when I take things personally that I really shouldn't. There are still times when I tend to walk this journey ahead of God, only to find out that I have taken a wrong turn, lost precious time, and have to be re-directed by Him, my Navigator. It is then that I am reminded that He is the Leader of my life and if I go where He leads, I will not get lost or fall by the wayside because He will never leave me nor forsake me.

So, if you ever see me behaving a little less virtuously, don't condemn me, just know that I am having a human moment and must be "going through." My spirit is very willing, but at times, my flesh is a little weak. However, I will continue to "study to show myself approved." I will continue to grow in order to fulfill my Creator's purpose for my life which is to coach, educate, and uplift people, particularly women and help them to live their own lives on purpose. If you are a child of God, a sister or brother in Christ, consider sending up a prayer for me…all godly prayers are appreciated. (If not, please don't bother.) Know that I am praying for you as well.

I hope that you have been blessed in some way by this book, my gift to you. If you have been blessed, please share it with someone. Remember to participate on my blog at http://JoyCDaniels.com , share the blog posts that you like, and sign up for my mailing list. More products will be available soon to guide you on your journey to virtuous living.

Take care, continue to strive to live virtuously each and every day, and keep in touch!

Joy C. Daniels

Addendum: I'd like to thank Ruth Abebe for her editing services and her patience. I'd also like to thank Qiana Fountain of Zuri Creative Services for her beautiful artwork used for the cover of this book. Additionally, I'd like to thank Omisade Burney-Scott for being the muse for the artwork. Fabulous women you all are! I appreciate the generousity of your time and talent. Many blessings to you all!

www.ingramcontent.com/pod-product-compliance
Lightning Source LLC
Chambersburg PA
CBHW060945040426
42445CB00011B/1012